Humony
Leadership

MINDSETS, SKILLS AND BEHAVIORS
FOR BEING A SUCCESSFUL
PEOPLE-CENTRIC LEADER

Steven Howard

Caliente Press

Humony Leadership
Mindsets, Skills and Behaviors
For Being a Successful
People-Centric Leader

Published by:
Caliente Press
1775 E Palm Canyon Drive, Suite 110-198
Palm Springs, CA 92264
www.CalientePress.com
Email: steven@CalientePress.com

Cover Design: Héctor Castañeda

Dear
Francesco,

Thank you for all your hard work
and dedication over the last
10½ years! Your development and
capabilities to grow and develop
the team around you are fantastic.

Keep up the great work.

Good luck and best wishes

Bev.

Contents

Foreword...7

Introduction 11

A Pivotal Moment for Organizational Leadership 21

The Need for Harmony. The Need for Humony. 37

Humony and Humony Leadership 61

Emotional Intelligence Empathy and Compassion 89

Dealing With Uncertainty and Ambiguity..............................111

Resilience 127

Adaptability.. 147

Tenacity.. 159

Building Strong Relationships 171

Wellbeing and Stress Management........................195

Cooperative Collaboration....................................239

Lifelong Learning..253

Creating a Humony Climate. Leading a Humony Culture.......277

Benefits of Humony 309

Quotes Related to Humony Leadership 313

Steven Howard Quotes on Leadership 319

Acknowledgments 321

About the Author...323

Dedication

For Adriana

Thank you for your love and support.

Without your encouragement and belief in me,
this book would never have seen the light of day.

Your love has touched my heart,
boosted my confidence,
and made me a better person.

For that I thank and love you eternally.

Our deepest fear is not that we are inadequate.
Our deepest fear is that we are powerful beyond measure.
Marianne Williamson

Some men see things as they are and ask "Why?"
I dream things that never were and ask "Why not?"
Robert F. Kennedy

Your greatness does not need to be proven.
Only exhibited.
Steven Howard

Foreword

L eading and managing talent has always been difficult, but today we seem to be facing a multitude of new and unique challenges simultaneously.

Think about it, in the past few years, leaders have been thrust into learning how to manage people remotely, how to build trust with more dispersed teams, how to hire people they have never met in person, and how to communicate and build culture with staff who are in more remote locations than ever before.

Leaders have also faced a rise in turnover and employee disengagement. In the past two years, 20% of the US workforce has voluntarily resigned, which is a record amount for any two-year period since the tracking of voluntary resignations began. While clearly, the pandemic has created some big new challenges, the complexity of what it takes to lead people and teams successfully has steadily risen the past few decades.

As the advancement of technology continues to disrupt how work is done, leaders have increasingly been faced with the challenge of upskilling their teams and working hard to make sure they are hiring and building the right skills for a future of work that seems less and less certain. And while the world of work is transforming, as this book goes to press, supply chains have been massively disrupted by Covid, the price of oil and gas has been significantly shaped by the war in Ukraine, and the prospect of a prolonged economic recession is very real. In short, we are facing one of the biggest leadership challenges in history.

While a great deal has been written about how the world of work has been transforming and how the pandemic has impacted both leaders and work, most of the discussion has centered around solving the challenges of today vs helping leaders in a more systemic and sustainable manner. This is why Steven Howard's work here is so paramount and so important.

Steven presents us with a bold new model of leadership built for a world where change and disruption are constant. Rather than present us with a complex leadership model rooted in machine learning, technology, and AI, in *Humony Leadership*, Steven delivers something far more essential and far more powerful. *Humony Leadership* is a leadership model based on our innate human capabilities and on our universal desire for harmony. Rather than razzle-dazzle us with some new "black-belt" type of leadership model borne out of some Ivy League think tank, Steven delivers something far more practical and relevant.

Leaders today are facing a moment of cognitive dissonance in that most schools and firms are still teaching models of leadership built for times when things did not change as rapidly as they do today. Most legacy leadership models strive to achieve control, consistency, and reliable outcomes. As we all have come to realize in recent years, in a world where so much is unknown and the pace of change is relentless, what we really need is a model to help us expect change and instability.

Humony Leadership is powerful because it helps leaders learn to harness opportunity in all this change, how to inspire without promising certainty, and how to lead with a sustainable human mindset. *Humony Leadership* recognizes the world of work is more fluid today and less predictable, and it helps you find your footing in a way that inspires you and those around you. At the core of this model is something every human can relate to: trust. In a world of constant change and disruption, what people want more than anything is to be in an environment of trust, working with people they trust. Steven lays out how leaders can realize this worthy destination

If you are like so many leaders out there today who are feeling the frustrations of working with stale and outdated leadership models, then you have come to the right place. In a world where work is changing quickly and where jobs are changing even faster, we deserve a new model of leadership that is in sync with these new realities. *Humony Leadership* is a refreshing and bold framework sure to help aspiring leaders today and tomorrow.

Steve Cadigan
LinkedIn's First Chief HR Officer
Workquake: Embracing the Aftershocks of COVID-19 to Create a Better Model of Working

Introduction

We cannot go back to the pre-pandemic methods of leadership and decision-making. The world has changed too drastically since March 2020. Hybrid work and working-from-home are now acceptable (and for many desirable) alternatives to the five-day, show-up-at-the-workplace workweek. And the need for more inclusive decision-making and leadership has never been greater.

Additionally, the rapid technological advancements of recent years make it impossible for individuals and organizations to predict what technical skills will be needed in the future. However, it is obvious that the so-called "soft skills" are now mandatory for organizational and personal success.

These are now Essential Skills. Or you may think of them as Powerful Skills. The skills for leadership success in the future are not technical; they are behavioral. And these skills are far from soft. In fact, they are highly multifaceted, take months to inculcate and learn how to apply, and are continuously evolving in scope and implementation. These skills are a complex collection of mindsets, capabilities, experiences, and personal attributes.

Undoubtedly, too many companies and organizations face a future in which their current business models are obsolete. As are their leadership practices and behaviors. Additionally, their leadership bench strength is woefully inadequate, ill-equipped, and significantly undertrained to handle the challenges and opportunities they will encounter.

The leadership skills needed for the post-pandemic period include a greater emphasis on ten core skills:

- Emotional Intelligence
- Empathy combined with Compassion
- Resilience
- Dealing with Uncertainty and Ambiguity
- Adaptability
- Tenacity
- Relationship Management
- Cooperative Collaboration
- Wellbeing & Stress Management
- Lifelong Learning (for both self and others)

These skills are now urgent. They are no longer optional. They are no longer "nice to have" skills in your leadership tool bag. They are now mandatory. At all levels of all organizations.

Future success means putting people before results. This does not mean a focus on people instead of results. Just a shift in priorities. Leaders must become people-centric first, then results driven.

We also need to redefine what "success" means and looks like, with the new definition requiring much more than financial results. Organizational success must now include creating new structures and sustainable working environments incorporating hybrid and work from home (WFH) scenarios, agility, and adaptability. They must also become places that support and enhance mental, emotional, and physical wellbeing. This is what future success entails.

Creativity, innovation, communication, and adaptation remain critical to forging strong organizations and robust economies. These will not be brought forth by artificial intelligence, the metaverse, or outdated leadership mantras and mindsets. Only an empowered and motivated human workforce can create these. As such, being fundamentally human and people-centric as a leader have never been more essential in the workplace.

Leaders must learn how to develop mindsets enabling them to confront and handle uncertainty and ambiguity. Neither uncertainty nor ambiguity should be considered obstacles. Both are permanent components of the post-pandemic period that need to be included in strategic planning and leadership mindsets.

This has tremendous consequences for the future of work. Uncertainty is one of the most challenging psychological events to experience. It is a natural human desire to want to feel certain about things in order for us to feel more in control. Yet, we cannot control uncertainty and ambiguity. Being able to cope with uncertainty and ambiguity is now a highly marketable leadership skill.

Humanize, Harmonize, and Futurize Your Organization

I call this new approach Humony Leadership:

> **Humony Leadership** – a created word combining *Human, Humanity*, and *Harmony* to emphasize the leading of people and the need for leaders to create workplaces of wellbeing and harmony.

Managing people is a 1980s construct. It is no longer applicable or relevant in today's world. It is why people leave bosses, not organizations. As U.S. Navy Vice Admiral Grace Murray Hopper brilliantly stated, "*You manage things. You lead people.*"

Additionally, leaders need to forget about the idea of control. Control went out the window in 2020 with the lockdown-mandated work-from-home environment. This means that leaders have to change how they trust and lead people.

It also requires a mindset and verbiage change from seeing employees as staff, assets, or resources to seeing and understanding them as human beings. And this means increasing respect in the workplace. Leaders need to understand that they must start first by trusting and respecting their team members (and not expecting automatic trust or respect based on titles or a position on an organization chart). After all, you cannot have harmony without trust and respect.

Will this be easy? No.

But it need not be difficult or expensive either.

As John Keynes wrote, "The difficulty lies not so much in developing new ideas as in escaping from the old ones."

A New Leadership Mindset

We have a broken mindset about leadership, one focused primarily on outputs and results. Our leadership models are designed to thrive in times of consistency and predictability. These models worked when organizational power smothered workforce choices and people's attitudes on the importance of work dictated perceptions of self-worth and self-image. Those days are history.

The Humony Leadership model is designed to enable leaders and organizations to thrive in times of uncertainty, ambiguity, and unpredictability. In other words: today's world. This model focuses on building working relationships and cooperative collaboration environments that empower people (and organizations) to thrive and flourish together in harmony and collective purpose.

The old mindsets and models of leadership will continue to work – but with cots and harmful ramifications for organizations, leaders, employees, and society that are not necessary. Humony Leadership is a far better methodology for achieving outcomes and producing results in the new realities of today. Organizations, societies, and – most importantly – our human workforces will benefit significantly from working environments of harmony and humanity.

The choice is yours. Remain comfortable with your old ways of leading, but pay the costs of high employee turnover and low employee engagement. Or aspire to be the leader and human being your people, family, and community needs for the workplace – and your corner of the world – to become harmonious and thriving places.

Why Become a Humony Leader?

Why should YOU become a Humony Leader? There are a multitude of reasons:

> It is time to change how people are treated at work by management, bosses, peers, and colleagues.
>
> The world needs more harmony.
>
> There is more to life than work and business results.
>
> The world needs more kindness and understanding.
>
> The world needs less divisiveness, anger, and separation.
>
> Humony is not exclusively for the workplace. These are life skills and usable in personal lives as well as within the workplace.
>
> Creating a better world for our children and grandchildren to inherit.
>
> We need more positive examples in society. Humony Leaders will be such examples, both inside and outside the workplace.
>
> To create a better world, we must be better leaders, better people, and better people leaders. This starts with Humony Leadership.

This is a better way to lead. To be a better leader. To make a difference at any level of any organization you have the opportunity to lead, now and in the future And, it is one that makes you a better human being while attaining the results you desire. The greater you understand this, the greater will be your impact on the organizations and people you lead, today and well into the future.

It Starts With You

The purpose of this book is to start a dialogue. First, within your thinking about your leadership mindsets, behaviors, and skillsets. Then, with your colleagues and peers. Followed by action, both individually and collectively. Progress does not happen without action.

Fortunately, many leaders – particularly in the frontline trenches – have the mindsets, skills, and behaviors of Humony Leaders. These are the leaders people want to follow. These are the leaders people want to share their ideas, concepts, and creative thinking with. For these leaders, this book is a reconfirmation that you instinctively are doing the right things. The ideas, actions, and behaviors found within this book will help you lift your game higher.

For leaders unsure how to adopt to today's New Abnormal, this book shows you how to become a more respected, successful, and awesome leader and person. You have the core skills in place, but your results focus is overwhelming your humanness. And people today need leaders who bring their humanness to their leadership roles. For you, the core concepts of this book cannot be understated: you need to unlearn management and relearn to be human.

These Humony Leadership skills will bring out the greatness within you. And they will enhance your ability to deliver sustainable and desirable results. Plus, there is a surprising hidden benefit in all this: you may actually start liking yourself better and enjoying your leadership responsibilities more.

My deepest wish is that this book, and the Humony Leadership concept, will propel you into becoming the leader – and human – that your organization, family, and community need. In doing so, you will also help the world become a better place for our children and grandchildren to inherit.

Great Leadership is an art. It is the art of achieving progress through the involvement and actions of others. This is why great leaders are strong in both leading people and leading for results, while good leaders typically lead only one or the other.

Humony Leadership provides you with the mindsets, skills, behaviors, and actions that will make you a great leader. A leader who is admired. A leader who is trusted. A leader that people look to for motivation, coaching, and direction. And a leader destined for a rewarding and fulfilling leadership career.

There is greatness within you. There has never been a better opportunity for you to exhibit this greatness. To paraphrase my favorite leadership philosopher (Yoda), *May the Force of Humony Be With You.*

Best wishes for continued success,
Steven Howard
August 2022

Leadership Defined

What is a leader?

In this book, a leader is defined as anyone who directly or indirectly leads people. Full stop.

This includes managers, supervisors, team leaders, first-line leaders, second-line leaders, and those higher in the organization. It also includes entrepreneurs, whether yours is a one-person business or a growing start-up.

I take the definition of a great leader to a higher echelon. I define Great Leadership as *the art of achieving progress through the involvement and actions of others*. Great leaders are strong in both leading people and leading for results, while good leaders typically lead only one or the other.

In truth, everyone is a leader, if only to motivate and lead themselves. Thus, every Individual Contributor should consider themselves a leader as well. And each of you is capable of becoming a Humony Leader.

The mindsets, skills, and behaviors in *Humony Leadership* will also serve you well in your personal life. Whether you are a parent, involved in community groups, or volunteering as a youth sports coach, *Humony Leadership* will help you in your endeavors.

CHAPTER 1

A Pivotal Moment
for
Organizational Leadership

Only three things happen naturally in organizations:
friction, confusion, and underperformance.
Everything else requires leadership.
Peter Drucker

The global business environment was changing before Covid. But now, the change is escalating at warp speed. We are in the throes of a pivotal moment, facing the greatest transformation in how we work since the early days of word processing and the desktop computer.

The past few years have been a challenge...for leaders in organizations, businesses, and government entities. And actually, for everyone else also!

A global pandemic. Cascading climate disasters. Escalating social and political unrest. Around the world. Combined with a growing distrust of leaders across all institutions.

Is this a time to shake up organizational structures and leadership mindsets? Or merely a temporary period to get through and revert as quickly as possible to the old ways of running organizations and making decisions?

Around the world, leaders, already stretched in all directions, have never faced so many dilemmas to reconcile, disruptions to navigate, and contradictions to adjudicate. Beyond dealing with the familiar aspects of their businesses, they now have to cope with the most fundamental human and organizational issues: health, wellbeing, safety, the Great Resignation, operating structures, business processes, and, in some cases, financial viability.

And the trade-offs are excruciating. Answers appear to conflict with each other, leading to decisions that are likely to be wrong. Many leaders believe they must return to business as normal in order for their industries, communities, and economies to survive. But the very act of returning to familiar ways of working could inhibit the ability of their organizations and entities to succeed long into the future.

Today, successful leaders must become skilled at dealing with an unending parade of apparent incongruities to thrive in this rapidly and constantly changing world. They must have strong convictions to confidently implement clear strategies and execution plans, combined with the calmness and readiness to recognize when circumstances necessitate a change in course or modifications in execution. This requires being adroit in creating strategies with built-in variations and the humility to understand that their predictions of the future have less certainty and accuracy than ever before.

They must build upon the processes, procedures, decisions, and traditions that made their organizations and teams successful in previous years. At the same time, they must vigorously embrace a new leadership ethos and implement new working structures that enhance cooperative collaboration among their team members and external partners.

They also must become adept at including and evaluating widely differing viewpoints, ideas, and opinions. This is particularly important for strategy implementation and incorporating innovative ideas and thinking on how work and tasks get done. Of course, this requires a large dose of humbleness and recognizing that the leader does not always have the optimal answer or the best idea.

It is time for massive change. Some leaders are waking up to recognize this fact. Others are stuck in their hopes for a return to the pre-pandemic normal.

A New Status Quo

For decades, businesses have operated with a set of industrial age values and capitalist imperatives where it has been acceptable, financially rewarding, and celebrated to exploit workers, natural resources, political systems, and even our planet. This has been the basis for the global economy, often giving business leaders more power and control than national or local government leaders. Even illegal and immoral behavior has been deemed an acceptable risk by leaders and managers. Many of these acts went undetected or unpunished, encouraging others to engage in such behavior. Long-term repercussions for the health and wellbeing of humanity and Planet Earth have been ignored or shuttered aside under the guise of increasing shareholder value and executive bonuses.

Fortunately, many also surfaced in recent years and resulted in fines and other punishments at such stalwart firms as Volkswagen, Wells Fargo, HSBC, Deutsche Bank, Toyota, Tesco, JP Morgan Chase, Barclays, Pacific Gas and Electric, Honda, Citibank, Dow Chemicals, Terminix, BP, Uber, Goldman Sachs, Toshiba, Deloitte, Bank of America, Fiat Chrysler, and Comcast.

Partially thanks to the pandemic, we have reached a reckoning. Like the dawn of a stunning sunrise, people are awakening to the fact that it is time for a change. It is time to reinvent the materialistic basis of our economies. It is time to rethink how people are treated at work by management, bosses, peers, and colleagues. Much like the days of segregation and apartheid, a psychologically unsafe workplace is no longer tolerable or acceptable. It is time to align economic growth with global progress and prosperity, ecological balance, and the destruction of social barriers.

This is not a utopian dream. The world was nearing a breaking point prior to the Covid pandemic. Now this change is underway and moving as if on anabolic steroids. Bold leaders will inspire and lead their teams and organizations to the right side of history and ahead of their competition. Others will lag behind until this new reality smacks them bluntly across their organizational hierarchies, silos, and balance sheets.

The first sign of this mammoth change is the willingness of people to quit their jobs, often without other employment lined up. But we cannot simply blame this on employee dissatisfaction or the sudden urge to continue working from home. Blame also needs to be laid at the feet of organizations and industries that made poor decisions in the early stages of the pandemic. And with those doing so now as the pandemic wanes.

For instance, the airline industry, which laid off thousands of workers as travel reached a near standstill during the pandemic, was hampered by a lack of skilled staff as business and personal travel rebounded. Shortages of pilots, cabin crews, counter staff, and maintenance personnel have resulted in tens of thousands of flight cancellations across the globe since the summer of 2021. Despite billions in government assistance programs, the short-sighted decisions to lay off staff resulted in a slower rebound for the industry as airlines had insufficient staff and capacity to handle increased customers.

Added to this are the new corporate policies regarding returning to the workplace. It used to be that employees left managers and bosses, not organizations. While still true, employees now are leaving organizations due to unacceptable policies on returning to the workplace, working from anywhere rules, and the sharp decrease in employee development due to budget cuts during the pandemic. No wonder employee loyalty has swung dramatically toward anything (and any organization) that can help ensure they remain relevant and employable in what is definitely an uncertain future.

Today's Reality

An interesting word aptly describes much of the global workplace environment, both pre- and post-pandemic: *omnishambles*. The word is compounded from the Latin prefix *omni* (meaning "all") and the word *shambles*, the term for a situation of total disorder. It also describes situations where poor judgment or mismanagement results in disorder or chaos with potentially disastrous consequences.

The global business world is suffering through disorder and disarray while being battered by confusion and chaos here in 2022. We are definitely in a period of omnishambles!

It is painfully obvious that pre-pandemic modes of operating and managing are no longer working for a large percentage of the knowledge workforce. Hence the en masse quitting of jobs known as the Great Resignation. The Great Resignation of 2021-22 has delayed post-pandemic rebounds for numerous organizations as they lose talent across the board. After all, it is very hard to grow your business when one of your top priorities is replacing lost employees.

The pandemic has increased the need for more meaning in people's lives. It is no longer enough to toil for a salary while living and enjoying life only on the weekends and paid time off. Fatigue has increased from all the uncertainties surrounding the pandemic. And purpose, especially purpose derived from work, has decreased.

When polled in September 2021, 24% of Americans reported they wanted a job "with more purpose," and 20% said they wanted "to step back from career and focus on personal life." In essence, people have become fundamentally different human beings due to how the pandemic was handled by government and business organizations. And there is no going back. This Great Awakening is a major contributing factor to the Great Resignation. It is also shaping the future of work in ways we are still trying to understand.

One's job or career path has long been a means of cultivating identity and self-worth, a way of striving for personal fulfillment and purpose. But the isolation and economic upheaval wrought by the pandemic have prompted a moment of mass reflection.

Over two years since the first office closures and economic shutdowns, we are in the throes of a widespread rejection of many of the old ways of working. Employees across the globe are quitting their jobs in record numbers.

Plus, many who have not quit are grappling with the question of how to make a living without their jobs defining their lives. And almost everyone is clamoring for greater work/life harmony.

Coming out of the pandemic, organizational leaders have three choices:

- Attempt to revert to pre-pandemic models of organizational hierarchies, vertical functionalities, and employees returning to the physical workplace environment with the majority working five-day, 40+ hour weeks in co-located offices, laboratories, and factories.

- Accept the need for some form of hybrid working

arrangements for a portion of the staff while keeping current organizational reporting and functionality structures in place.

- Adapt to the new opportunities emerging from the pandemic to create flexible organizational structures that are agile, adaptable, and flexible.

Humony Leadership will prove more valuable and beneficial in each scenario than results-only driven leadership practices characterized by stagnant information flows, top-down directives, unacceptably low employee engagement, and escalated levels of stress, burnout, and mental exhaustion.

Welcome to Your New Organization

Every organization is effectively a new organization. The past is prelude. You cannot return to your former mindsets and behaviors as a leader. Those need to evolve and be built upon. The past is a foundation, not a destination to restore, revisit, or recreate.

Every employee is effectively a new employee. Why? Because it is a new environment (continuous pandemic or post-pandemic). We have not been here before. So, you have to define how you will rejuvenate working together, no matter the size or structure of your organization.

Everyone needs to be re-onboarded into your new organization, some of them remotely. Another new skill leaders need: building trust with people you have never met other than via a video call.

Leading remote staff was thought to be a temporary skill at the pandemic's start. It is now a permanent skill encompassing work from home, work from anywhere, hybrid arrangements, and a variety of permanent, temporary, irregular, and transitory employment situations.

The pre-pandemic model of the organization-employee relationship was that organizations bought the employee's time (usually 8-5) and mandated that this daily time slot, five times a week, be devoted solely to them. Handling personal business or concerns during the working day was considered anathema and barely condoned, even for the most urgent personal matters. Plus, employees were told where they would physically be placed to spend this time sold to their employers.

The new model for the employee-organization relationship (note that now the employee comes first in this equation) is that the organization is buying a skill set and, in many cases, the purpose and passion of the employee. Together, the employee and the organization will decide where they work best and how best to deliver their commitments and responsibilities to the rest of the organization and its customers.

The best outcomes will be produced when the employee has work/life harmony and integration, including a say in where and how they can best perform their duties and responsibilities.

With this new model, both the employee's and the organization's long-term and short-term perspectives and goals become combined, connected, and harmonized.

A New Model of Leadership

Managing people is a 1980s construct. People do not want to be managed. They want to be led. Being managed by an ill-equipped or coldhearted manager is why people traditionally leave bosses, not organizations.

Additionally, employees are empowering themselves. Empowerment is no longer only ordained by line managers and senior executives. Managers no longer control who receives empowerment and who does not. This is one more sign that control has gone out the window, especially in remote work environments.

The leadership skills needed for the post-pandemic period are not technical; they are behavioral. These Powerful Skills, such as emotional intelligence, empathy, compassion, resilience, adaptability, and tenacity, are now urgent. They are no longer optional. They are no longer "nice to have" skills in the leadership tool bag. They are now mandatory. At all levels of all organizations.

This approach is grounded in Epistemic Humility, which I describe as being humble with assumptions about understanding people, situations, events, and behaviors. It also starts with a commitment to stop judging others. Judging involves creating names, labels, and limited views we apply to people, places, and things. When we do this, we form an attachment to these ideas. Judging is managerial action. Understanding is leadership.

Humony Leaders seek to understand why their team members perform above or below expectations. Their attention is on processes, behaviors, emotional states, and actions. Being future-focused, such leaders use motivational and effective feedback techniques to encourage replicating positive performance or enhancing non-optimal performance.

Leaders with a Managerial Mindset, on the other hand, focus on results and outputs. Thus, they judge behaviors, emotional states, and actions. Their focus is on present states and conditions; without long-term context or consequences in mind.

Managers deliver blame or praise as they determine appropriate based on their judgments and the likelihood of immediate impact. While desired short-term results may be attained, the longer-term consequences on employee morale, engagement, and retention are costly.

I call this new approach Humony Leadership – a created word combining *Human*, *Humanity*, and *Harmony* to emphasize the leading of people and the need for leaders to create workplaces of wellbeing and harmony.

People want to feel good when working (note: work is no longer a place one goes to, but the tasks one does). To feel good, they need four things:

- To be respected and trusted
- To be accepted for who they authentically are
- To be included in discussions and decisions
- To have responsibilities and assignments that lead to personal and professional growth

What one skill brings all four of these needs together? Harmonizing.

Humony Leaders resemble orchestra conductors who harmonize the skills of their musicians while adapting to changing acoustic environments. Humony Leaders are adept to adapting to changing economic and workplace environments. They bring harmony to their workgroups and workplaces.

Harmonizing means being connected with your people, colleagues, and peers (and everything going on in their lives). Success requires harmonizing everything impacting the short-term and long-term sustainability of the business. It takes the creation of a Harmony Mindset in everyone from frontline supervisors and managers to the C-suite.

Another key aspect of a Harmony Mindset is having a longer-term perspective regarding the people you lead. This includes new thinking on your relationships with them and your responsibility for their continued growth.

Steve Cadigan, author of *Workquake: Embracing the Aftershocks of COVID-19 to Create a Better Model of Working* and the Foreword to this book, has a deep-seated belief that melds well into the Humony Leadership approach. As you know, current leadership models focus on how to lead people when they are working for us.

However, as Cadigan notes, even within the confines and constraints of these models, great leaders continue to lead, guide, and mentor people long after they have stopped working directly for them.

Cadigan believes such actions are important and critical traits of successful people leaders. Why should leadership and mentoring stop when someone leaves for another team or manager? Or even when they leave for another department or company? They should not.

As Steve wrote to me, *"This is wrong. Mentoring and coaching should always continue. Doing so benefits both parties. Plus, it is more human, honest, and harmonious with life."* I could not agree more.

In my career, I continued mentoring and coaching several people after they had left the organizations we were working for. These activities often continued for more than five years after their careers took them elsewhere. Even better, the relationships and friendships with these people lasted for decades.

I fully support Steve's thinking and encourage you to do so as well. Doing so is an important part of the developing people responsibilities discussed later in chapter 12. This is not only about the future of work. It is also about the future of life.

To create harmony in our lies, we must think beyond leadership only in our workplaces.

The Future Is Now
Humony Leadership also requires a mindset and verbiage change from seeing employees as staff, assets, or resources to seeing them and understanding them as human beings (with lives and responsibilities outside work).

This approach results in greater revenues and reduced costs (including absenteeism, workplace conflict, course corrections, and workplace-related medical expenses). This translates into either more operating and investment capital, or profits, depending upon how leaders decide to utilize these increased cash assets.

If you do not implement this leadership approach, your very survival is at stake. This applies personally at the individual manager and leader level and financially at the organizational level.

This approach is needed at every level of all organizations. Having Humony Leaders at the top and dictatorial managers in the first-line and second-line leadership ranks is ineffective. In many ways, leaders need to unlearn what they have learned and practiced to succeed post-pandemic.

Hence, this approach now becomes a corporate culture and workplace climate issue, requiring new thinking, behaviors, and best-practice actions to be cascaded throughout the organization.

However, even without this corporate culture inculcation, leaders who utilize this approach within their departments or teams will reap the rewards for their business units, including lower employee turnover than the rest of the organization. They will also personally benefit by being seen as successful and top leaders by others within their organizations, including senior management.

And, perhaps best of all, this approach will help leaders become better people, parents, partners, and human beings!

All of the great leaders
have had one characteristic in common:
it was the willingness to confront unequivocally
the major anxiety of their people in their time.
This, and not much else, is the essence of leadership.
John Kenneth Galbraith

CHAPTER 2

The Need for Harmony.
The Need for Humony.

To handle yourself, use your head;
to handle others, use your heart.
Eleanor Roosevelt

Coming out of the pandemic, there is a growing desire for harmony in people's lives.

Forget work/life balance. People need work/life harmony. And they need harmony in their workplaces. And in their personal lives.

Harmony is not a concept or description often applied to the workplace. But it should be.

Think about what it means to be in harmony. Things are flowing, either personally or collectively. If the latter, it is like a well-oiled machine humming along frictionless. When this happens, you are in sync with what you are doing. You are so fully in being with the moment that time disappears. You are becoming the moment. There is a sense of oneness with the moment and with your task. This is often referred to as a "flow state." In flow, you find synchronicity with people, events, and things. You feel your best and are performing at your best. One might even consider this an optimum state of consciousness, but that is a topic for another book!

Harmony in the workplace is more than the absence of conflict. And it is greater than joyful camaraderie. It is higher than people merely getting along to accomplish tasks. Workplace Harmony is when people cooperatively collaborate, share information and ideas, help one another out, have each other's backs instead of back-stabbing, and enjoy contributing to an identified team or purpose.

In such an environment, things are running smoothly and change is viewed as a necessary (and welcomed) ingredient for continued progress.

A State of Rudeness

Unfortunately, almost all workplaces are sadly distant from anything remotely considered harmonious. Almost everyone I talk with about their work environment scoffs at the notion of it having harmony.

Research from McKinsey identifies one of the reasons for this sad state of affairs: rudeness. Their study revealed that nearly two-thirds (62%) of employees are treated rudely by colleagues at least once a month. This includes being insulted, interrupted, put down, dismissed, or having crude language directed their way.

There is more than just an emotional cost to this bad behavior. Managers and employees who feel disrespected tend to perform worse, sometimes on purpose! A full 80% reported losing time at work worrying about disrespectful incidents. And 63% said they lost time at work avoiding their offender.

When people feel disrespected or are subjected to rudeness, their motivation wanes. They also start questioning whether their workplace is the right environment for them. The natural reaction to being treated negatively is to reduce engagement, collaboration, information sharing, insights, and ideas.

Most damaging, at least to their organizations, 48% reported intentionally decreasing their work effort after being treated rudely and 38% admitted to intentionally decreasing the quality of their work.

Without a doubt, uncivil treatment by bosses or colleagues is one of the many factors contributing to the Great Resignation. And most often, those who quit due to experiencing bad behavior tend not to notify their organizations of this contributing factor. Hence, what employers are unaware of they cannot fix. This leads to further staff resignations due to an uncivil work environment and the continued toleration of rudeness by those who remain.

Toxic Cultures

A toxic culture was the single best predictor of employee attrition during the first six months of the Great Resignation – ten times more powerful than how employees viewed their compensation in predicting employee turnover. In an article in the MIT *Sloan Management Review* (January 2022), the authors of a research study into the causes driving the Great Resignation wrote, "*the leading elements contributing to toxic cultures include failure to promote diversity, equity, and inclusion; workers feeling disrespected; and unethical behavior."*

The five most negative toxic culture attributes were cited by the researchers in a subsequent MIT *Sloan Management Review* article in March 2022:

1. Disrespectful
2. Non-inclusive
3. Unethical
4. Cutthroat
5. Abusive

Disrespectful was defined as a "lack of consideration, courtesy, and dignity for others." The non-inclusive factors included inequities related to LGBTQ, disabilities, race, age, and gender. It also included cronyism and nepotism. The cutthroat element included backstabbing and ruthless competition, while the abusive definition included bullying, harassment, and hostility. I suggest that micromanaging is another significant contributor to many toxic workplace environments.

None of these elements are acceptable in today's workplaces, and none should be tolerated, no matter what results are produced by those contributing to or causing a toxic workplace environment. It is little wonder that a report from the Society for Human Resource Management (September 2019) stated that 20% of employees leave a job at some point in their careers because of a toxic culture. That is truly deplorable.

There is a cost to employee unwellness and organizational profitability from toxic workplace atmospheres. Numerous research studies show that a toxic workplace is associated with increased burnout, stress, and both physical and mental wellness issues. Additionally, according to an article in *Management Science* (February 2016), "*when employees experience injustice in the workplace, their odds of suffering a major disease (including coronary disease, asthma, diabetes, and arthritis) increases by 35% to 55%.*"

Of course, when toxic cultures make employees ill, health costs go up. By one estimate, toxic workplaces were responsible for an incremental $16 billion in employee health care costs. That is a tremendous hit on corporate profitability.

Microaggressions are another contributing factor to toxic workplace cultures. These microaggressions can debilitatingly impact people's sense of being seen, heard, and understood at work.

Microaggressions come in many forms, including racism, sexism, ageism, ableism, and many others. Do not dismiss these by focusing on the "micro" part of the word. Understand the impact of the "aggression" part of the term.

Microaggressions are anything but "micro" in terms of their accumulated impact on the emotional and mental wellbeing of those targeted. The slights, demeaning comments, and nonverbal displays of eye-rolling and shaking of heads all add up. Being repeatedly dismissed, alienated, insulted, and invalidated builds up over time and creates many problems related to low sclf-csteem, exclusion, wellbeing, and mental health issues.

It can be uncomfortable to know that we may be complicit in microaggressions in the workplace, unknowingly or simply through the fear of speaking up. However, every time we allow a microaggression to occur, we send the individual on the receiving end a reinforcement that their safety is less valuable than our comfort. Such silence also buttresses the biases creating microaggressions.

"Biases are the root of many microaggressions – little, everyday slights and insults – often unintentional that make another person feel belittled, disrespected, unheard, unsafe, othered, tokenized, gaslighted, impeded, and/or like they do not belong," writes Melinda Briana Epler in her book *How to Be an Ally: Actions You Can Take for a Stronger, Happier Workplace.*

Each of us needs to take a proactive approach to recognizing and stamping out microaggressions in the workplace. Reducing microaggressions will help create harmony within the workplace climate. Doing so will also create safer, more inclusive, diverse, and equitable workplaces.

As discussed in chapter 13, leaders are responsible for the workplace climates within their workgroups. Toxic cultures are more likely to be found at the workgroup level than at the corporate culture level. With that said, however, the corporate culture can highly influence the workplace climates across an organization. However, the bottom line remains: you are responsible for the workplace climate within the part of the organization you lead or influence.

Create a Harmony Mindset

Managers and leaders often want people and teams they can control. Finding and having these is less likely than ever before. If you can forget about the idea of control, this will change your approach and mindset on how to trust and lead people.

As in all Humony Leadership skills, the first place for creating a Harmony Mindset is to start with yourself. How are you contributing to any disharmony in your workplace? What are you doing to promote harmony within your team and between the various functional areas with which they work or interact?

Likewise, become aware of your biases. We all have biases – some of which are helpful though the majority are not.

Interestingly, most biases are negative. They produce negative thoughts, emotions, and behaviors. Biases are learned responses and behaviors, which means they can be unlearned with conscious effort.

Which of your biases are negatively impacting your work relationships? Which prevent you from showing empathy or compassion to any of your team members? Which cause you to like or favor any particular team member(s) over others?

For each of these questions, the primary follow-up question is: why?

The second step is observing the interactions of your team members.

What needs to be harmonized within your team and why? Start with analyzing your workplace climate, the working relationships between members of your team, and the work/life harmony of your team members.

Then, expand your thinking to how well your team members work with other areas of the organization. What needs harmonizing between your team members and those in other functional areas (or customers) with whom they work or interact? Review the questions above and apply them individually and collectively to those reporting to you.

The third step is evaluating how harmonized your team is. How are these pieces fitting together? What do they and you need more of and less of? Where is there (negative) tension with your teams, processes, policies, and procedures?

What feels or looks out of balance? Is the imbalance temporary, or is it becoming a new status quo? Adjust, adjust, and readjust like the experienced sailor (leader) you are. Experienced sailors are in harmony with the winds and the currents.

This is not a time for checklists. It is a time for holistic observation and understanding. It is a time to meld your gut instincts and your rational thoughts.

This is best implemented at every level of the organizational hierarchy. If you are a senior leader in the organization, the questions you should be asking are:

> How well are your leaders harmonizing at their levels?
>
> How well are they ensuring their direct reports harmonize the next level?
>
> How proficient are they at turning internal conflicts into collaboration?
>
> How well are they balancing the human costs

(including mental, emotional, and physical wellbeing) with the achieved results?

Are they taking into consideration the toll on employee mental, physical, and emotional health as they drive their teams to higher levels of performance and results?

How are they managing and reducing burnout rates, errors caused by fatigue, and emotional meltdowns?

How are they creating harmony between cross-functional work groups and their teams?

If you are not a senior leader, these are the same questions you should ask yourself.

Harmonizing Mindset

Having a Harmony Mindset means constantly monitoring the workplace climate, the feelings of individual team members, and the communications, workflows, and interpersonal relationships of your team members. Reviewing and discussing these should be a vital component of your one-on-one discussions with those you lead.

It means you go from focusing only on results and outputs to contemplating the human impact from how those results are produced. What are the human or wellbeing costs associated with those results? What is the cost to your human workforce and their wellbeing?

One way to cascade the Harmony Mindset among your team members is to get them to describe a toxic workplace culture. Then design a workplace climate that is 180 degrees opposite. Here are the common elements of a toxic workplace climate:

Lack of respect from managers or colleagues

Bullying

Focusing only on results

Workloads causing stress

Interactions with co-workers causing stress

Lack of support from direct manager/supervisor

Managers spending more time in meetings with fellow managers than in conversations with their staff

Directive and controlling

Inflexible rules on when/where to work

Limited chances to contribute ideas or suggestions

A Harmony Mindset means you quickly want to fix or change anything out of kilter. But in doing so, you must ensure you do not overreact to every situation and event. Ask: is it an incident or a sequence? Incidents can be overlooked. Not every situation needs to be turned into a learning opportunity. We all have bad days and moments. On the other hand, sequences must be stopped if they are disruptive or negatively impact performance.

My personal rule is that three occurrences constitute a sequence. If someone speaks abruptly to a colleague, that is an incident. If they do so twice within a short period (say within four weeks), my internal radar goes on high alert. If it happens a third time, that establishes a sequence and means it is time to take action and prevent further instances from occurring.

Remember, you cannot have workplace harmony each and every minute of every day. A harmonious workplace is an ultimate goal, like world peace. Do your best to nurture a harmonious workplace environment. Nip incidents not conducive to this in the bud as early as possible.

As a harmonizing leader, you will react with kindness, empathy, and compassion, responding as a leader, coach, or mentor. Doing so will add to a workplace climate of harmony. However, if you react with anger, sarcasm, yelling, threats, and verbal abuse, you will be responding as a manager, bully, or jerk and helping to create a toxic work environment. The choice is yours. As is the choice of humans to decide in which environment they prefer to work.

Workplace Harmony

Harmony in the workplace used to result from conformity. Everyone was listening to the same music, so to speak. The routines of the workplace environment created the "music of harmony" within the workgroup.

That is now gone. As a result of working from home, many people are now listening to their own music (thoughts), and harmony via conformity has disappeared (along with managerial control).

So how do leaders bring their team members into the virtual or hybrid building under a harmonized roof? It must start with trust and respect. Additionally, leaders must learn to create, build, and maintain trust and respect with new hires (or new teams) that they have not met face-to-face. That requires a heightened level of trust in others that will be uncomfortable for many.

Respect and trust are the two foundational elements of Humony Leadership. Please do not interpret this as the respect you believe you are due as a leader because of your title or position. It is actually the opposite. It is the respect that you show as a leader to those reporting to you, as well as to your peers, colleagues, business partners, customers, and all others.

This is a mindset change. You have to earn respect as a leader by showing respect to others. And by creating a respectful and harmonious working environment for those you lead.

Hence, workplace harmony comprises five overlapping elements:

> Respect
>
> Inclusion
>
> Belonging
>
> Conflict management
>
> Cooperative collaboration

These are the five elements in the workplace that need harmonizing.

What might Workplace Harmony look like? In most cases, workplace wellness, leaders displaying empathy and compassion, and inclusion will all be in evidence. There will be a focus on converting workplace conflict into collaboration. Leaders will "walk the talk" regarding wellbeing and bring revitalized energy to the workplace and their teams. Steps will be taken to reduce work-related stress and burnout. This will result in greater employee engagement, productivity, innovation, and solutions that produce increased business results.

Such workplace harmony will not be achievable all the time. That is fine, as long as a harmonious workplace remains the vision. Without a doubt, you will experience periods when:

- People feel lost
- Stress will happen
- Anxiety and uncertainty will be unavoidable

You cannot create a permanent, idealistic environment. After all, you are dealing with people, and we humans all have our ups and downs. But a harmonious workplace is the destination. When you get off course, knowing your destination enables you to amend actions, behaviors, and communications to get you and your team back on track.

Fortunately, the resiliency and agility built into a harmonious workplace will enable leaders and team members to bounce back quicker and stronger when these unharmonious periods arise. We all have bad days and "off" days. That is part of life. But resilient people bounce back quickly from their off days and place greater focus, energy, and effort into their good days.

Additionally, when people are triggered, they are not likely to deal effectively with conflict, be open to new ideas, exhibit curiosity, or be creative or innovative in solution ideation. An environment of harmony provides a safe space to express ideas without fear of retribution. It also creates additional capacity for creativity and innovative thoughts by keeping negative emotional triggers at bay.

People also need a sense of belonging. What's the link to bringing everyone together into the virtual building? Harmony.

Harmony is like a magnet. Both see increased bonding when distance is reduced. Even when physical distance cannot be reduced, connectivity distance can be minimized. This happens through respect, inclusionary practices, and focusing on making your people a priority over results.

One quick and easy way to bring harmony into your team: put an immediate end to negative personalizations and characterizations of people by members of your workgroup.

After all, having experienced two-plus years of a global pandemic impacting everyone's lives, why would you allow anyone in your workgroup or organization to speak negatively about, or to cast aspersions on, another human being? Of course, this has to start with you. So, no more talking about the "nerds in IT" or the "bean counters in finance."

Put an end to defamations that promote stigmas and deleterious stereotypes of any subset of the human race. No more crass jokes. No more sexual innuendos. No more toxic comments about anyone's political, sexual, or religious persuasions. No more cultural typecasts. Tell your team members clearly that you will no longer tolerate these comments. Starting today. Right now.

This standard may seem a bit like the search for world peace. It may never be attained, but it is certainly worth striving toward. And, of course, we will all slip up. None of us are perfect. However, handling such slipups – in others and ourselves – with compassion, understanding, and fortitude will go a long way in inculcating this behavior. And doing so will help to reduce the many microaggressions taking place throughout the workplace.

Aim for harmony, not happiness. Happiness will result from a harmonious environment.

Belonging

Belonging is a core human need that drives many of our behaviors and desires. It also enhances the meaning of life and fuels many of our deepest emotions. Researcher Dr. C. Nathan DeWall claims, *"Humans have a fundamental need to belong. Just as we have needs for food and water, we also have needs for positive and lasting relationships. This need is deeply rooted in our evolutionary history."*

In 2009, the Centers for Disease Control and Prevention (CDC) identified increasing a sense of belonging to be a matter of disease control in schools. I see no reason why the same would not apply in the workplace.

Fostering a culture of belonging in your organization is critical with the rise of hybrid work. Remote working strained the bonds of trust and connection, even for teams that were in good shape before the pandemic. Additionally, new employees who were onboarded remotely in the past two years have not been able to fully develop important connections with their colleagues.

Belonging is not a behavior that can be demanded or required. Belonging is subjective because it is based on each individual's perceptions at any given moment. Feelings of belonging or not belonging are transient. Leaders need to create a climate of complete inclusion within their workgroups. The stronger the climate, the less transient the sense of belonging. Feelings of not belonging are normal, commonly experienced, and easily overcome in the right workplace climate.

Famed psychologist Abraham Maslow stipulated that a failure to satisfy the need for belonging results in maladjustment and emotional distress, forcing people to invest their energies in meeting this deficit rather than in higher-level thought processes. In other words, deficits in a belonging culture impact productivity, innovation, and creativity.

True belonging requires authenticity and vulnerability. But many workers do not feel that they can be either. One Harvard study found that over 60 percent of employees feel pressured to conceal some facet of their identity at work. Suppressing or obscuring personal traits or individuality was highest among LGBTQ (83%), Black/African Americans (79%), women (66%), Hispanic/Latinx (63%), and Asian/Pacific Islander (61%) groups. Even 45% of heterosexual white men often feel they have to cover up their age, disabilities, or mental health concerns.

Feelings of not belonging also often result from people believing they are not heard. Or that their opinions and views do not matter to others. Having ideas rejected is frightening. People often do not speak up because of the uncertainty of how others in a group may respond. If there is a lack of trust in openly discussing ideas, people will shut down and not contribute.

George Orwell coined the phrase "groupthink" in his book *1984*. Groupthink occurs when the desire for social conformity takes place at the expense of open discussions. To avoid conflict, people avoid expressing opinions, sharing data, or voicing ideas that depart from the group's collective beliefs or thinking. The result is an environment in which only collective agreement is acceptable. Such groups become resistant to new evidence and innovative thoughts, leading to a lack of critical analysis and poor decision making.

The need for belonging is so strong that people often prefer not to share their thoughts, ideas, and beliefs to retain group membership and peer approval and avoid possible conflicts. They will go to the extreme of self-censoring their comments, even to the point of not speaking up at all. Here are some of the thoughts that go through their minds:

> Should I say something?
>
> Will I be ridiculed?
>
> Will I be blamed if my idea does not work?
>
> Will everyone understand the experiences I have had?
>
> Are my thoughts relatable to the person talking?
>
> Will there be retribution?

To overcome these fears, there must be a climate of zero tolerance for retaliation, scorn, mockery, and ridicule. Leaders must create a climate of certainty that all team members will accept all ideas at face value before discussing and evaluating them. There can be no automatic dismissal of ideas or suggestions (a best practice of brainstorming sessions).

Leaders must encourage everyone to speak up, participate in discussions, and share their ideas and thoughts. Not speaking up should not be an option. Of course, this requires a psychologically safe work climate, a topic I will address later in the book.

Drop DEI

Leaders, particularly at the frontline team level, need to build workplace climates comprising inclusivity and belonging. The entire team must accept and welcome each other, not just the leader. The leader can set the tone for belonging, but they must also work to ensure all team members are likewise exhibiting behaviors of belonging to each other.

One major problem with DEI programs is that they are seen as initiatives, which means they are perceived as temporary. Important today, shelved later.

The word diversity focuses on our differences as humans, and DEI programs aim to smooth over those differences under the moral umbrella of inclusion. That leads to reluctant acceptance of having to include everyone and listen to everyone's ideas.

As a better alternative, the Humony framework would encourage you to change your Diversity, Equity, and Inclusion programs to Human, Equality, and Inclusion. Scrap the emphasis on diversity and focus instead on inclusion and belonging. Do not aim for equity – focus on equality.

Doing so rightly places the focus on inclusiveness, not diverseness and diversity. A focus on equality, which is easily understood by all, is preferable to the numerous definitions and perceptions of equity. Plus, equity focuses on trying to create a new balance in an attempt to right the inequities of the past or present. Equality starts with a clean slate that is comprehensible to all and is future focused.

A Human Equality and Inclusion mindset starts with the moral underpinning that everyone in the workforce (and society) is equal, a much better platform for gaining true inclusion and fostering collaborative input and output. Today's diversity programs tend to focus on inclusion based on race, gender, sexual identity, and those with special needs. Human Inclusiveness is more (and better) than DEI, as it embraces everyone, including those from different cultural backgrounds, introverts, new hires, and remote workers.

Speaking of remote workers, there is no excuse for allowing proximity bias to impact inclusiveness. These are your people. Be proactive in taking steps to weed out proximity bias. Thinking that this is an unresolvable issue means thinking that past ways of job assignments, promotions, and rankings will suffice. They will not. Just as we have overcome previous constraints in the workplace (segregation, child labor, lockdowns), leaders can proactively figure out how to eliminate proximity bias.

The key is not how often your employees are in the office, but how proficient leaders are at optimizing interactions, deepening relationships, and building trust through all their interactions, including co-location, virtual, and remote.

Full inclusion is a byproduct of acceptance. Everyone needs to accept others as humans on their own journeys in life. The workplace is only a part of their journey. As such, everyone has responsibility and accountability for not engaging in behaviors, actions, expressing opinions, or participating in conversations that are upsetting or demeaning to others.

This also applies to those who do not lead people, such as individual contributors and those working in manufacturing facilities. They need to be coached and counseled that disrespectful, divisive, and exclusionary behaviors, words, and actions are no longer acceptable. The false camaraderie of workplace cliques that exclude others can no longer be tolerated or justified by "that is the way things are done here." Anything that produces an "us vs. them" attitude, behavior, or communication must be eliminated.

Inclusion must be a proactive process. As Stephen Frost, founder of the UK firm Included, wrote, "*Unless you consciously include, you will unconsciously exclude.*"

Spiritual Nature of Humans

Humans have innate spirituality. We are spiritual beings having a human experience with a sentient body. So why not bring this spiritual aspect of our human beingness into the workplace? Why force people to leave their spirituality at the door when entering the workplace? Doing so creates a lack of whole-person harmony in the working environment.

We need to recognize that spirituality is an aspect of the whole person. We cannot ask people to "bring their whole selves to work" and then ask them to leave their spirituality at the workplace entrance.

Perhaps it is time to accept and acknowledge spirituality in the workplace, which is the concept that humans are not physical beings on a spiritual journey but rather spiritual beings on a physical journey. Allowing spirituality – not religion – into the workplace could activate greater kindness, respect, tolerance, and acceptance of one another as human beings.

Admittedly, this is a difficult subject to raise – but we do a disservice to ourselves and others if we do not recognize this truth, no matter a person's theology or perspective on life. There is no need to overtly promote spirituality in the workplace; just allow it to happen. Do not cut it off or hinder it.

I am specifically talking about spirituality, not religion. And I realize the statement that we are all spiritual beings in a human form may not be recognized and accepted by all. But it is becoming an accepted belief, including within many religious organizations.

Religions divide. Religion is exclusionary and creates out-groups. Spirituality is inclusive. It is common to all of us, crossing all cultures, races, and geographies. It does not need to be promoted in the workplace, just accepted and tolerated. But we cannot fully lead, coach, and mentor people if we ignore their spiritual inclinations and beliefs.

Unfortunately, discussing the spiritual aspects of being human is not common in the workplace. Even the concept of mindfulness is stripped of its spiritual component and reframed for the workplace in terms of increasing productivity and reducing stress.

In the early stages of mankind, our spirituality was strongly valued (as it still is in so-called "ancient" cultures). It is time to allow this fourth dimension of being human to be included in workplace discussions with our other three dimensions – body, mind, and emotions.

On the other hand, you do not need to call it spirituality if doing so will cause problems or is culturally unacceptable. Call it humanity. If parents and schools are deficient in teaching and instilling humanity in our younger generations, then humanized workplaces need to pick up the slack.

The Spiritual Being is part of the Whole Being, a core component of humanity and what it means to be human. It is part of the mystery of being alive.

Why can airports and hospitals have non-denominational worship rooms and not workplaces? Be non-descriptive if necessary: solitude rooms, mental break rooms, quiet rooms, etc.

Interestingly, the "break rooms" at work have historically been central locations for food and beverage. But, just as people need to refuel their bodies, they also need to refuel their brains and spirits. Why not break rooms for the brain and soul instead of just for the stomach?

Benefits
The benefits of creating a harmonized workplace climate include:

1)   Create more harmony in everyone's life

2) A better way to lead and grow your team

3) Enhances your career by building a reputation and track record as a people leader producing recognizable results

True leadership power is the ability to bring peace into your workplace (and your life) while progressing toward desired results and outcomes.

Read the next chapter to learn how Humony Leadership is a different, more powerful, and more beneficial way to lead.

The task of leadership is not
to put greatness into humanity,
but to elicit it,
for the greatness is already there.
John Buchan

CHAPTER 3

Humony and Humony Leadership

Leadership is all about people.
It is not about organizations.
It is not about plans. It is not about strategies.
It is all about people motivating people to get the job done.
You have to be people-centered.
Colin Powell

Across the globe, we live in divided societies and cultures. We have too many "*Karens*" espousing verbal abuse at people of color. Too many passengers yelling at fellow travelers and airline staff, often using brutal words of hate. There are too many police officers forgetting their jobs are to "protect and serve" not "punish and pummel."

Too many cable anchors ridicule and mock one another while searching for ratings and advertising revenue. In doing so, they break the cardinal rule of journalism about not becoming the story.

We see too many people blasting others on social media for holding views contrary to their own. Anyone can become a keyboard warrior spouting hatred and ridicule left and right. At times, it seems like the whole world is speaking, but no one is listening. Emotion-laden verbiage and labels are spewed, overwhelming any attempts at rational discussion or discourse.

All this social conflict and discord is also visible in organizations and workplaces. As Gregg Ward, Founder and Executive Director of The Center for Respectful Leadership, notes, "*anger and animosity are at higher levels than at the peak of the Vietnam War. And they are prevalent in almost every medium-size or large-scale organization.*"

A growth mindset means you are open to everything and permanently attached to very little. While it is a natural desire to hang on to what we have, this is extremely risky in today's turbulently changing world. A natural reaction to the end of the pandemic is to grasp onto and clutch the so-called New Reality we are currently witnessing. But it is not the right thing to hold onto. A Newer Reality will replace it in time to come, sooner than most people expect or want. This is why I label our current workplace climate the New Abnormal.

As a result, organizations with unchanging thinking about leadership are unprepared to cope with four growing problems generated by the changed thinking of their workforces:

Trust – people no longer want to work for bosses who do not trust them.

Workplace Wellness – people no longer want to work in organizations that do not support their mental wellbeing, especially those with highly stressful work environments.

Work/Life Harmony – people no longer want working arrangements that are not conducive to their non-work-related responsibilities and priorities.

Fear of Returning to Old Routines – people are not keen to return to work situations that are demotivating, uninspiring, and psychologically unsafe. Especially work environments causing disengagement with co-workers, dissatisfaction with their jobs, and emotional stress. They know what this feels like and, with many other options available, they do not want to return to these toxic environments.

One silver lining from the pandemic, for many, is the realization that they have choices and greater control over their employment arrangements. It also means that leaders and managers must change their mindsets about what it takes to be successful people leaders. Likewise, leaders and managers need to grow and develop new skills and behaviors to become people-centric leaders.

Leaders can stanch the impact of the Great Resignation by creating workplaces of dignity, opportunities, equity, and harmony. This will be true human-centered leadership.

The New Abnormal

Accelerating change, numerous global challenges, shifting expectations, and transformed mindsets about work are the foundations of the New Abnormal. Added to this mix is the Great Disconnect between the workforce and leaders. And even between leaders and their self-concepts. There is no playbook for the period we are entering. It is little wonder that leaders struggle to know how to lead in this environment.

There is no Old Normal to return to. It is long gone. There is not even a firm New Normal beneath our feet. Today is the New Abnormal – the biggest global and human reset in history. Fortunately, it is also where the opportunity and chance to begin anew with a more human approach to business and interacting reside.

Many leaders instinctively suspect that reverting to prior leadership systems, mindsets, behaviors, and actions will have minimal impact in today's New Abnormal. But with what do leaders replace old habits, mindsets, behaviors, and set ways of operating?

There is a tremendous need to reinvent how we lead and work together. For all leaders, this is an opportunity to create healthier and enhanced work environments where human ingenuity, creativity, and collaboration can produce stellar, sustainable results.

In recent months, much has been written that the key to success is changing corporate cultures to be more aligned with purposes the workforce can identify with. That is all fine and dandy. But without better equipped and skilled leaders in place, such purposeful corporate cultures merely become passive mission statements lacking motivational impetus and long-term meaning.

Here's the key: culture matters...leadership matters more.

Success in the New Abnormal requires reframing how leaders lead, from frontline managers and supervisors to the C-suite leaders. Change the way leaders think and lead – and the culture and workplace climate will change for the better.

Leadership is not a one-size-fits-all formula. But there is a foundation for building and enhancing your leadership skills, mindsets, and vibrancy. It is time to refine your craft of leadership based on the people-centric principles of Humony Leadership.

Leaders are not broken. Organizations are not broken, just not built and structured to handle today's challenges. Current structures devalue mental health and self-care. And they do little to generate and sustain the need for balance and harmony.

If you think you will return and operate your business or business unit as if it is February 2020, you will get crushed, both organizationally and professionally.

If you think you lead the same workforce as before the pandemic, you are wrong. If you think you will be leading people with the same mindsets, the same mentalities, the same desires, and the same priorities as two years ago, you are badly mistaken.

The uneasiness you feel about being a leader today is not your fault, especially if instinctively you know there must be a better way to lead your people through the corridors of ambiguity and uncertainty. Most likely, though, a piece of you has gotten lost in recent years. This resulted from focusing on managing people and pushing for results instead of being human. It happened from working in a culture that values productivity over human wellbeing.

You have three choices: change, step aside as a leader, or retire. There is no going back. There is no Old Reality to return to. The role of a leader is no longer to be a task overseer and a reporter of results. Rather, the leader's role today – at every level of every organization – is to be a people performance coach.

Change how you think and lead, and you will change the corporate climate and workplace culture for the betterment of all your stakeholders. Doing so will also convert the abnormal into your new normal.

Who benefits from this leadership approach?

- Team Members – by being treated as humans and not staff or "resources"

- Organizations – through reduced employee attrition, absenteeism, presenteeism, and associated medical and insurance costs

- Business Results – through greater creativity, productivity, and employee engagement

- Leaders – through attaining greater results and more harmonious workplaces and an increase in leadership wellbeing

- Society – through an increase in kindness and a decrease in public displays of incivility

- You – by producing greater results and advancing your career (and by becoming a better human being in the process)

The bottom line is that the skills, mindsets, and behaviors of Humony Leadership will create better leaders. And better leaders create better workplace cultures, better organizations, better lives, and better humans.

On a personal level, Humony Leadership will propel you into becoming the leader – and human – that your organization, family, and community need. In doing so, you will also help the world become a better place for our children and grandchildren to inherit.

Why Humony

Humony is a people-centric approach to leadership. Today's managers and leaders have demonstrated the ability to achieve business goals, but they are not trained to lead or develop people for today's evolving circumstances.

Putting people first requires protecting and caring for employees (as human beings, not just workers). This comes from understanding how employees feel and what they think about their jobs, workloads, work/life harmony, and personal responsibilities. Of course, these feelings and thoughts are constantly changing based on their personal situations, challenges, and opportunities. Hence, this is not a once-a-year, tick-the-box activity.

Traditional leaders often ask: is this quicker? Is this more efficient? It is now time to ask is this humane? How will this impact the human population comprising our workforce? How will this affect the responsibilities that our human employees have outside the workplace, such as parental, home schooling, community involvement, personal wellbeing commitments, or the need to attend to elderly parents?

One lesson from the pandemic: people want greater human connection. Leaders need to excel at the human connection aspect of leadership. Good bosses care about people when they work for them. Great leaders care about people for their entire careers, even when these people move on to other organizations.

Top-down leadership is outdated, counterproductive, and demoralizing. As Dan Gable, professor of organizational behavior at London Business School, wrote in the *Harvard Business Review* (April 18, 2018), "*By focusing too much on control and end goals, and not enough on their people, leaders are making it more difficult to achieve their own desired outcomes. The key, then, is to help people feel purposeful, motivated, and energized so they can bring their best selves to work.*"

Stop treating employees as only a means to an end. This mindset is contributing to millions of people worldwide quitting their jobs and seeking new employment with organizations that value them as human beings. There has been a fundamental change in what people value, and work is no longer the most important thing that defines a large portion of the workforce.

While employers may want to revert to the days of the hard-working ethic culture that built vibrant economies, robust organizations, and elevated executive compensation into the stratosphere, this is not going to happen. That is incompatible with a workforce that now treasures wellness, meaning, and harmony over paychecks that increase a few percentage points above annual inflation rates. Working harder and longer is no longer worth sacrificing or deprioritizing health, harmony, personal relationships, and nonwork responsibilities.

Humony Leadership is not about people over profits. It is about putting people <u>before</u> profits. People over profits is either/or. People before profits means people + profits.

Organizational and team goals are unlikely to be met when employees are distracted by personal, emotional, mental wellbeing, or other cares and distractions. Employees' feelings affect all aspects of organizational processes, procedures, outputs, and results. Plus, emotions and feelings impact the workplace environment, wellness, conflict, and collaboration. Leaders can no longer focus only on how employees think and behave. They also must understand what and how team members are feeling.

And leaders have to place greater emphasis on the professional and personal growth of themselves and their people. As author and consultant Tim Leberecht wrote, *"Humans will only thrive if we keep investing in what makes us inherently human: vulnerability, empathy, intuition, emotion, and imagination."*

Creativity, innovation, communication, and adaptation remain critical to forging strong organizations and growing economies. These do not result from processes, procedures, or policies. They result from attracting, retaining, and motivating exceptional and engaged talent.

This means understanding humans, the nature of humanity, and being fundamentally human have never been more essential for leaders to be successful in the workplace.

The Humony Framework

Humony provides a framework of specific areas for leaders at every level of organizations to focus on to create sustainable results and businesses.

The Humony Framework tackles and resolves five critical issues that are a carryover from the pre-pandemic era:

Soft Skills Mentality – thinking that "soft" skills training is optional and not vital for success. Today, nothing is further from the truth for supervisors, team leaders, managers, and seasoned executives. And the same applies to Individual Contributors who need to collaborate and interact with others.

Focusing Only on Results is Driving People Away –the unrelenting push to deliver greater results, without considering the impact on the mental and physical wellbeing of team members, has millions of workers re-evaluating their priorities. Results are important. So is increased productivity. But not at the expense of stress-driven health issues.

Leaders Uncertain Where or How to Change – fears of being seen as "soft" or "weak" have prevented many leaders from showing their human sides. Plus, their hard-nosed, unemotional methods have successfully driven results throughout their careers. Why should they change now? Because the world has changed and how people view work/life balance and work/life harmony has changed.

Gap between what Employees Want and what Leaders Think They Should be Doing – leaders think they should be managing their direct reports while employees would rather be led. No one goes to work hoping to be micromanaged. No one wants to work for a boss who does not trust them or who keeps them on a short leash. No one wants to work in a place where disrespect, bullying, and rudeness are prevalent. Many managers have been promoted through the years because their command-and-control approaches drove results. Control went out the window in 2020 when work-from-home became the norm. Employees want trust, respect, and a say in how they get their work done. Leaders who think they can return to their old methods when people return to the workplace will pay a price.

Workplace Conflict and Low Employee Engagement – while conflict in the workplace continues to rise, employee engagement continues to ebb and flow at unsatisfactory low levels. Anyone who thinks these two trends are not interlinked is misinformed. And both are tied to the push to continuously deliver greater results and surpass goals and metrics handed down by senior management.

These are issues found at all levels of organizations. Thus, they are solvable at all levels of organizations.

While many are created by the attitudes and actions of senior leadership, they are best resolved at the frontline, team, and department levels. This is why the Humony Framework and the Humony Mindset are for everyone who leads people, not just those in the C-suite dictating strategies and policies.

The answer lies in creating working environments (offices, hybrid, remote) that are thriving places of connection, wellbeing, collaboration, and creativity. Innovation and productivity – however you choose to measure these – will ensue and likewise thrive.

Being successful in doing so starts with understanding what your team members want and desire.

What Employees Want and Need for Success

Covid-19 was a comet leading to the destruction of stuck-in-the-mud dinosaur leaders and organizations not listening to what employees want and need.

People want to work for organizations where they are truly valued, cared for, and feel they belong.

A survey from the Society for Human Resource Management (SHRM) released in August 2020 showed:

- 84% of U.S. workers blame poorly trained managers for creating unnecessary stress.

- 57% say managers in their workplace could benefit from training on how to be better people leaders.

- 50% felt their own performance would improve if their direct supervisor received additional training in people management.

The study also cited the top five skills people managers could improve. These were: communicating effectively (41%), developing and training the team (38%), managing time (37%), delegating (37%), and cultivating a positive and inclusive team culture (35%).

Numerous other studies substantiate these survey results. For instance, the December 2021 DDI Frontline Leader Project reported that 57% of workers quit a job because of a bad boss.

And in October 2021, a survey from Robert Half of 2800 office workers in 28 cities reported that 49% of employees said they had quit a job to escape a toxic manager.

Additionally, more than three-quarters of employees said their managers have "glaring flaws," according to a 2019 survey from VitalSmarts of over 1300 employees. Respondents said their managers are overwhelmed and inadequate (27%), poor listeners (24%), biased and unfair (24%), distant and disconnected (23%), and disorganized and forgetful (21%). None of these surveys paint a very good picture of the worldwide state of management and leadership.

A key human need is a sense of agency, or the power to decide. Research shows people are more engaged, committed, and productive when they believe they have a choice in how they carry out their work responsibilities. Self-determination theory suggests that people are motivated by three innate and universal psychological needs – competence, relatedness, and autonomy. When these three needs are fulfilled, people are more motivated.

When people are allowed to make even small decisions, they start to feel like they have "skin in the game," a feeling that increases engagement and the desire to work toward a collective outcome. The greater the decisions, the greater their personal investment in the task, project, and push for the desired outcome.

Other research has shown a strong link between autonomy and productivity. Employees and teams with a high sense of autonomy tend to be more innovative. This is partially attributable to having greater persistence in overcoming problems on the projects they control.

Too many managers believe they have to micromanage individuals and teams in order for work to get done. However, given the brain's innate drive and desire for autonomy, this approach usually backfires. Empowerment is not giving employees free rein. It is, however, giving them agency and autonomy, combined with trusting they will do their best. That is a powerful combination.

Control and micromanaging result in compliance and no more than reluctant acceptance to tackle a task as mandated. Autonomy results in engagement, cooperative collaboration, and higher levels of buy-in.

Also, employees want to be heard. In the days of office-based organizational structures, the standard internal feedback techniques were the annual employee satisfaction surveys and the old suggestion box. Try using either of these with success in today's hybrid workplace environment. When everyone was working in the same place, a quantitative assessment of the workplace environment was a good start. It has little applicability when people work from home, in remote locations, or via a mixture of on-site and remote flexibility.

Today, you need to measure employee satisfaction with their leader's effectiveness in creating a workplace environment of inclusiveness, belonging, and wellbeing.

In Gallup's global study of nearly two million employees, one of the key findings was that approaching employee feedback and engagement as a sporadic or annual HR measurement task is a big mistake.

Research by the Gartner Group shows a dramatic disconnect between the perspectives of leaders and staff. An amazingly high 77% of executives believe their employees have opportunities to give feedback on how to improve their work experience. In stark contrast, only 40% of their employees share the same perspective.

Earlier in the book, I mentioned four things that people need to feel good when working:

- To be respected and trusted
- To be accepted for who they authentically are
- To be included in discussions and decisions
- To have responsibilities and assignments that lead to personal and professional growth

This essentially boils down to treating them as human beings and ensuring they feel they belong on your team, department, organization, or company. People need to feel good to be successful. If you make them feel good and they have a sense of belonging, they are more likely to take pride in their work. They are also more likely to contribute, collaborate, go the extra mile, and be innovative and creative.

Clear Line of Value

One additional factor people want and need to succeed is knowing how they provide value. People are more fulfilled when given a chance to contribute to a team's or an organization's success. Too often, however, leaders do not tell employees how their efforts provide value to a team objective, a department goal, or an organizational strategy. It is what I call a Clear Line of Value.

In recent months, a lot has been written about the need for organizations to emphasize corporate purpose and mission to connect with current and future workforces. And there is a lot to be said for this. Since the pandemic, people have been re-evaluating their purposes and priorities in life and the role that work plays in these.

While this is a great place to start to define and communicate the purposeful intention of the organization, mission and vision statements quickly start to wear thin. Especially when people do not understand their role or contribution in helping the organization, or the team, drive toward obtaining such objectives and goals.

The way to entice cooperative collaboration is by ensuring every individual contributor on your team knows and understands the value contributions they are making. This goes a lot deeper than being told they are "an important team member" or a "valued contributor."

Rather, leaders need to explain – and constantly reinforce – the specifics of how each team member adds value to a project, the team, a departmental goal, or an organizational strategy.

All employees should understand the Clear Line of Value they are providing. Otherwise, tasks become busy work. Jobs are viewed as personally unsatisfying. Personal motivation wanes.

Collaboration decreases as little value is perceived in cooperating.

Knowing that the work one is doing provides value is intrinsically motivating. Intrinsic motivation is much more powerful than extrinsic motivation. When you explain to people how their efforts provide value to other parts of the organization or customers, they become more fulfilled, energized, motivated, and engaged.

Not only should you regularly highlight this Clear Line of Value to your team members, but you should also have discussions about value contributions. Ask them, "where did you contribute a lot of value last week?" or "what value did you contribute to that project?" Are their responses in line with your observations? If so, reconfirm that their contributions were important and why. If not, add your thoughts and perspectives on their Clear Line of Value.

If people know their work is important and adds value, their engagement and productivity levels increase. Absent this knowledge, their jobs become dull, routine, and boring. And they tune out and disengage.

For these and many other associated reasons, one of the mantras I preached to my coaching and mentoring clients is very simple: Recognize Efforts. Reward Results. Far too many leaders, particularly first-line managers and supervisors, fail to recognize the efforts of the people they lead. They tend to recognize and reward people only when the results are tabulated. This is a mistake. Recognition of effort is critical. As is showing that such efforts are appreciated by you as their leader.

Appreciation and gratitude are two of the most important levers you have as a leader. As long as what you express, of course, is authentic. Insincere or tick-box expressions of gratitude and appreciation are more likely to backfire with unintended and undesirable consequences.

It may seem strange that receiving genuine and heartfelt messages of appreciation and gratitude from one's immediate boss is so motivating. Here is some research that may surprise you:

> A 10-year, groundbreaking study of 200,000 managers and employees by O.C. Tanner Learning group revealed that 79% of employees who quit their jobs cited a lack of appreciation as a key reason.

> That same study also disclosed that 65% of North Americans reported that they were not recognized *even once* by their leaders or supervisors over the past year.

This is why it is important to recognize efforts. Do not wait for the end results. Celebrating and calling attention to progress is a motivating practice. If you want motivated and engaged staff, ensure you continuously highlight to them the value of their efforts and outputs.

If you cannot define the value your team members are producing – individually and collectively – then perhaps it is time to re-examine what they are doing and why. If you cannot identify the value each person is producing, how can you expect them to? And, if you do not regularly communicate their value, do not blame them for losing sight of it and becoming disgruntled or disengaged. Leadership has responsibilities. And this is one of them.

It is little wonder that the Society for Human Resource Management (SHRM) said before the pandemic (2019) that only 38% of employees feel satisfied with their current job. As witnessed by the Great Resignation, that number has fallen significantly in the past 24-30 months.

Not surprisingly, the lack of appreciation has been cited as one of the top contributing factors in nearly every research study into the causes of the Great Resignation.

Humony Leadership Mindset
Humony is a better model for working with and leading people.

More than a framework, Humony is a mindset. A mindset that focuses on:

- People first, outcomes and results second
- Employees as human beings (with lives and responsibilities outside work)
- Harmony as a cornerstone of workplace environments
- Workplace wellness as a priority focus

Remember, you lead people, not organizations, workgroups, or teams. Also, you do not manage people. You manage processes, policies, procedures, projects, and things. A leader's role is to develop and grow people. Understanding this is fundamental to a Humony Mindset.

Another mindset change: employees (including gig workers and contractors) are the most important stakeholders for the organization's long-term success. Humans are not a cost to be contained but the main generator of value for the organization. Future of work strategist and author Heather McGowan says that 84% of the enterprise value of the firms in the S&P 500 is now created by human capital, with only 16% of the value being generated by physical capital. This is the polar opposite of the early 1970s when physical capital accounted for 83% of value creation.

The Humony Mindset comprises:

Harmony

Human Focus and Impact

Human Needs (respect, acceptance, inclusion, belonging, and growth)

Humanity Focus

This is not a check-box list. A Humony Mindset integrates these four components into how you think, behave, decide, and act as a leader. Consider these as your new set of leadership values. We can think of this as the new Triple-H Bottom Line: harmony, human beings, and humanity.

In terms of harmony, strive for frictionless cohesion within your team, across all work groups, in cross-functional interactions, and with the various internal or external customers your team serves.

Change your priority focus on decisions from desired outcomes to how each decision will impact your human workforce. Even better, change your thinking from workforce to human force. Your employees and team members are not workers; they are humans.

This is not a game of semantics. It is a serious mindset change, similar to what marketing-led organizations have done for years. Airlines serving customers far outperform their competitors handling passengers. Hotels with staff who consider their clients as customers provide better service than those seeing visitors as (temporary) guests or room occupants. People who buy services are customers, not patients, cardholders, clients, passengers, visitors, or account holders. Organizations that consider them as customers and treat them as such see increased customer loyalty and repeat business.

The same mentality now applies to your employees. They are not workers, staff, employees, associates, or team members. They are human beings. And, like all human beings, they want respect, acceptance, and inclusion. Your leadership mindset must integrate into this new reality. As do your leadership behaviors.

A Humony Mindset requires switching from thinking of employees as work-delivery systems to understanding and valuing them as distinct and value-producing individuals with personal needs, wants, desires, likes, and dislikes.

With a Humony Mindset, the criteria for decisions include a baseline encompassing:

> Does the decision respect our human workforce? Our customers?

> Does this decision exclude, segment, or segregate any portion of our human workforce?

Is this decision based on the inputs of the affected members of the workforce? If not, why and how will the consideration of their inputs be explained openly and transparently?

How does this decision impact humanity today and future generations?

How will this decision impact local communities and your organizational partners if implemented?

This is why I regularly repeat this mantra: you should not manage people; you must lead them. When you lead them appropriately, powerful results ensue. Like the inability to control individual drops of water in a river, you cannot control people. But you can maneuver those drops to collaborate and create a powerful force that produces a desired result, such as generating electricity or turning a windmill. The same goes for the humans comprising your team.

The final element of the Humony Leadership Mindset will fundamentally change your relationship with the people you lead. Toss aside the notion that your role as a leader is to get the most out of your people. That is 1990s thinking. It also leads to burnout, health issues, job dissatisfaction, and unmotivated human beings comprising the bulk of your staff.

While these have been noticeably present in most workplaces since the 1990s, they escalated significantly during the two-plus years of the pandemic.

Your job as a leader is to put the most into your people! And reap the benefits and rewards for doing so: increased productivity, employee engagement, a happier workplace climate, and reduced employee attrition.

By putting the most into your people, you will get the best out of them. This makes the continuous development of your people – through coaching, mentoring, motivating, and other methods – the number one priority for you as a leader.

Humony Leadership

For leaders, it is time to unlearn management and relearn to be human. Processes and procedures are great, but they can never be more powerful than being a human.

This makes Humony Leadership different from other leadership concepts that people talk about, such as servant leadership, heart-forward leadership, and heart-centric leadership.

Like those concepts, Humony Leadership also has a foundation of focusing on people first, bringing out the best in others, supporting those reporting to you, and exhibiting empathy. But Humony Leadership encompasses several other steps, including continuous learning for yourself as a leader, enabling people to bring their whole selves into the workplace, and the acute spotlight on creating harmonious workplace climates for the part of an organization under your sphere of influence.

The key is learning to lead people in both a human and a harmonious way. With some humility thrown into the mix. Being a Humony Leader requires not taking yourself too seriously and not trying to be perfect. No human being, including you, is perfect. Pretending to be so, especially to the people you lead or to your peers, automatically signals inauthenticity. And that, in turn, erodes trust, the very foundation of great leadership.

Model the skills of humony in your interactions with others. You do not need to lead others to do so. Lead yourself, your actions, and your behaviors with these skills, and you will find yourself immersed in a kinder, gentler, and more peaceful world. As Gandhi said, "*be the change you want to see in the world.*"

This approach is not solely for the first two to three years of the post-pandemic period. This is the next step in the evolution of leadership. But it will take courageous leaders to implement and stay the course long term.

You never get everything you want as a leader. But you do get what you choose. Choose to be human and you get humans working with you. Choose to show respect and you get respected. Choose to be trusting and you receive trust.

Another way of eroding trust is by micromanaging others. No one wants to be micromanaged. You can achieve more as a leader by micromanaging processes, not people. Micromanaging is often a behavior of those fearful of losing power or control. It is the same for managers who want all their staff to return to co-located facilities because that is the only way for them to exert power and control over what their employees are doing during the mandated working time slots. These are not leadership behaviors; they are managerial ones.

Here is an unfortunate example of this behavior:

Right from the start of our fifth session, the young

woman I was coaching was distraught and stressed. But she did not want to say why.

It was the fourth month of mandatory, work-from-home lockdowns. Despite the small size of their apartment, both she and her husband were coping well. Their only issue seemed to having to share the limited broadband connection.

She was the Communications Manager for a rapidly growing services company providing analytics and analysis to companies across a wide range of industries. She also headed the Professional Women's Employee Resource Group at the company.

Finally, I forced her to admit that she was carrying a burden that needed releasing. When asked to tell me her greatest challenge, she literally screamed in reply, "my micromanaging boss and his control-freak attitude."

This is a woman who wants to grow, both personally and professionally. So, when invited by other groups in the company to attend strategy discussions on how to help clients in those early days of the pandemic, she readily agreed.

Her boss, however, was not in agreement. He held a daily call with her in which he went over in detail the meetings she had on her schedule and the status of the projects she had going.

Even though she was on top of all her projects, he forbade her (his words) from attending any meetings not directly related to current assignments and projects. He "wanted her available, just in case anything came up" and did not want to "risk" her not being available if and when he needed any information from her.

Thus, instead of attending meetings in which she could have learned and contributed, she was forced to spend hours each day in "standby mode" with little or nothing to do.

Not surprisingly, as the pandemic came to an end, she sought and found other employment in a company that relished her enthusiasm for learning and growing. Last I heard, she was happier than ever at this new firm.

An ultimate win for her, a big loss for the company, which has seen other young and aspiring women move on to other opportunities as well.

Humony Leaders recognize that power, control, and competition do not equate to leadership. In fact, these attributes weaken leaders and their effectiveness. And, like any negative, downward spiral, weakened leaders typically resort to more power, control, and competition to negate or stem their weakening effectiveness. Without a doubt, it is a vicious cycle that many fall prey to.

By inculcating a Humony Mindset, people-centric Humony Leaders avoid the pitfalls that trip control-and-command, results-focused, numbers-driven leaders. This is what I mean by the phrase "unlearn management and relearn to be human." The best thing about being a Humony Leader is that you do not have to sacrifice results when being a people-centric leader. In fact, you are likely to achieve higher results in the long run from greater employee engagement, lower staff turnover, and increased innovation and creativity.

The foundation of the Humony Leadership approach is the understanding that innovation, creativity, collaboration, and productivity come from motivated and engaged people. For most leaders, productivity means creating additional output with the same resources.

But in a more harmonious working environment, leaders will likely create the same current output with less time, friction, and rework. This will create more time for innovation, thinking, and creativity.

That is true productivity, especially since the bulk of revenues for many organizations five years from now will come from products and services not currently offered. Those products and services will be born from innovation, thinking, and creativity, not from creating more output today.

We need more positive examples in society. Humony leaders can be such examples outside the workplace. They can show others how to show up in life.

Exemplifying humony outside the workplace will create ripples of humanistic and humane interactions. Your reward will be self-pride and perhaps a more civil society for your children and grandchildren to inherit.

We lead by being human.
We do not lead by being
corporate, professional, or institutional.
Paul Hawken

CHAPTER 4

Emotional Intelligence
Empathy and Compassion

Sharing emotions builds deeper relationships.
Motivation comes from working on things we care about.
Sharon Sandberg

As leaders begin to stage the return to the workplace, they have an immense opportunity to display stronger levels of emotional intelligence, especially empathy and compassion.

Emotional Intelligence is not a so-called soft skill. It is a hard-edge leadership skill that provides high-value and bottom-line results. It is the true affect and impact we have on those around us, a critical skill that brings out our best performance and allows us to bring out the best in those we lead and influence.

Effective leaders have something in common, and it is not technical skills or a high IQ. Research indicates that effective leaders have a high degree of emotional intelligence.

Daniel Goleman, the Rutgers psychologist and author of *Emotional Intelligence,* calls emotional intelligence the *"sine qua no of leadership. Without it, a person can have the best training in the world, an incisive, analytical mind, and an endless supply of smart ideas, but they still won't make a great leader."*

Emotional intelligence is the ability to understand and manage your emotions, as well as to recognize and influence the emotions of those around you. Leaders use their emotional intelligence skills to guide their behavior, enhance interpersonal relationships, and understand the behaviors and emotions of others.

It is a simple rule when it comes to your emotions: if you do not manage your emotions, they will manage you. Utilizing emotional intelligence skills puts you in charge, not your emotions.

Emotional intelligence makes it easier to take an honest look at oneself, identify strengths and gaps, and make the changes necessary for personal and professional growth. It provides us with actionable tools to better connect with colleagues and clients and make more optimal decisions under pressure.

Emotional intelligence also increases the tendency to ask open questions, actively listen, and admit to your mistakes. It also reduces the tendency to respond to situations impulsively.

Displaying emotional intelligence as a leader will not make you appear weak. Nor will it impede your ability to make tough choices or hold difficult conversations with team members, particularly underperforming ones. In fact, several studies have found a strong association between emotional intelligence, the capability to drive change, and the ability to provide visionary leadership.

Emotional Intelligence Is A Skill

We are all emotional creatures. It is what makes us human. What is the impact of this on being a leader? What is the impact of this on leading others?

To begin with, emotional intelligence is not about trying to remove or withhold your emotions. It is about understanding and managing the expression of emotions, both yours and others. On the other hand, autopilot mode is the antithesis of emotional intelligence. It prevents you from recognizing which emotions are driving behavior and decision making.

Emotionally intelligent leaders do not spend time on things they cannot control. Rather, they focus on what they can control: their attitude and how they use their physical, mental, and emotional energies.

Those high in emotional intelligence have an increased ability to generate optimistic thoughts and shutter aside negative ones. They use emotional regulation to put healthy emotions at the forefront of their mindsets. This enables them to prioritize long-term goals over short-term inconveniences, obstacles, and hurdles.

The benefits of emotional intelligence skills include:

- Improved emotional self-management
- Enhanced communication skills
- More adaptable and agile leadership behaviors
- Enhanced resiliency skills

- Increased overall optimism

- Decreased workplace stress

- Reduced interpersonal conflicts

- Stronger relationships, both professionally and personally

- Better personal wellbeing and mental wellness

- Achievement of career and personal goals

Here are some research findings that exhibit how important the skill of emotional intelligence (EQ) is for leaders:

- Global consulting firm TalentSmart tested Emotional Intelligence alongside 33 other important workplace skills. Their study concluded that EQ was the strongest predictor of high performance and accounted for up to 58% of success in all types of jobs.

- In a study by the Stanford Research Institute, conducted within Fortune 500 companies, researchers determined that 75% of long-term job success is contingent on people skills, compared to only 25% for technical knowledge.

- Another study from TalentSmart, of more than 2000 managers in 12 large organizations, revealed that 81% of the competencies that differentiated outstanding managers were related to EQ.

- A study of 44 Fortune 500 companies found that salespeople with high EQ skills produced twice the revenue of those with average or below average EQ scores.

- Research by the Human Capital Institute

uncovered a 31% increase in leadership development effectiveness in organizations when EQ is valued compared to organizations where EQ is not highly valued.

- In a study from Waterford Inc, companies led by people with high emotional intelligence reported, on average, 50% less employee turnover, 56% higher customer loyalty, and 38% above-average productivity. They were also 27% more profitable.

Core Competencies of Emotional Intelligence

The four components of Emotional Intelligence are self-management, self-awareness, social awareness, and relationship management. Not only is Emotional Intelligence an essential leadership skill, but it is also a highly valuable life skill as well.

Here is an overview of the specific competencies associated with each of the four components of emotional intelligence:

Self-Awareness

Recognizing and owning your emotions. Attuned to how emotions affect your thoughts, mindset, mood, behavior, actions, and words. And their impact on your job performance, decision making, and inter-actions with others.

Also, knowing your strengths and weaknesses. Which emotions are easier for you to manage? Which ones are likely to lead to outbursts? Knowing the things and people that trigger your positive and negative emotions.

Understanding what fuels your triggers, such as tiredness, stress, anxiety, lack of sleep, unresolved workplace drama, personality clashes, and personal issues.

Naming your emotions clearly to understand their roots. For instance, anger may result from a sense of deeper feelings, such as hurt, disappointment in others, displeasure in an unsatisfying outcome or circumstance, jealousy, or powerlessness.

Self-Management

Having the ability to control the expression of impulsive feelings and behaviors. Basically, not allowing an emotional hijacking to result in words, actions, or behaviors that you are likely to regret or negatively impact your relationship with another.

This is not to say you should bury your emotions. Rather, you need to manage the expression of your emotions. In other words, getting angry, mad, or upset about a situation is okay. But there is a huge difference between allowing an emotion to prompt you to throw an item across the room and saying to someone, "I am greatly upset by what you just said." Both are expressions of anger. The latter approach is much more appropriate and signals higher emotional intelligence and self-management of how emotions are expressed.

Leaders competent in this skill tend to remain calm under pressure and capable of maintaining an emotional balance, even when stressed. Self-control of emotions leads to clearer thinking in stressful situations. Under stress, the brain reverts to binary decision making, limiting your choices to two dissimilar pairs: this or that, A or B, black or white, option one or option two, etc. When you are in binary decision-making mode, the emotional control center of your brain (the amygdala) has taken charge. And decisions tend to be less-than-optimal.

By getting your emotions under control, you enable the rational control center of your brain (the prefrontal cortex) to take over. This enables decisions to become more rational and less emotional. The result is almost always a more optimal decision based on facts, asking better questions, and an improved analysis of the multiple options available to you.

Owning and managing your reactions to others. If someone is rude or negative toward you, reacting similarly rarely does any good. Chances are you will regret doing so, even if only in how you criticize yourself in your mental self-talk. Pause. Think. Reflect. What is the most appropriate and emotionally intelligent manner of responding? Walk away? Ignore? Both are valid options to consider.

Adaptability in expressing your emotions. Leaders proficient in adaptability handle many demands while staying focused on their most important skills and objectives. Being able to adjust suddenly to external changes or circumstances. Knowing that uncertainty is a given and being comfortable with this fact.

Social and Organizational Awareness

Attuned to the emotions and concerns of others. Understanding these without judgment, criticism, or praise. Realizing that others have responsibilities and ownership of their emotions and how these are expressed, just like you have ownership and responsibility for your emotions and how you express them.

Being fully aware of emotional cues in others, such as changes in voice tonality, body posture, word selection, or breathing patterns. Also, keen organizational awareness with the ability to recognize the power dynamics in groups, teams, or organizations, including knowing where formal and informal power and decision making is held.

All organizations have unspoken norms, in-groups, historical conflicts, and guiding values. Having a grasp on these, without becoming subdued by them, is advantageous for you and the people you lead.

Being attuned to interactions with others and if these are being affected by their emotions (or you). Understanding that how others interact with you may be dictated by how their emotions influence (or control) them. Being receptive to the social cues and non-verbal body language of others.

Negative signals include:

> Zero or minimal eye contact
>
> A faster pace of talking than normal
>
> Talking non-stop and refusing to yield
>
> Tightness in body posture
>
> Over-active hand gestures
>
> Fidgeting

Are these non-verbal signals triggering emotions in you? Are they impacting your ability to listen to what is being said – and not said?

Also, being consciously aware of what you are projecting with your own social cues and non-verbal body language!

Relationship Management

Knowing how to develop and maintain good relationships, both professionally and personally. This often leads to the ability to inspire or influence others, two powerful attributes of great leaders. Turning personal conflict between people into cognitive conflict about ideas, opinions, and choices. Working toward agreeable solutions to the benefit of the team and organization.

Those with strong relationship management skills usually work well in teams unless those on a team are low in emotional intelligence skills.

Strong EQ leaders exhibit an ability to bring people to shared perspectives, contexts, and conditions. They create an atmosphere where team members willingly commit to assisting and supporting the team's efforts. Building group belonging, identity, relationship growth, and the spirit of camaraderie and solidarity.

The ability to persuade and influence people to collaborate cooperatively, rather than forcing them into unsatisfying teamwork activities and projects. They build a workplace climate of cooperation, respect, and helping one another.

How you handle your relationships with others is the epitome of emotional intelligence. The Cardinal Rule of Emotional Intelligence: stop to think about how your words and actions will be interpreted and felt by others. You can start by asking yourself these six questions in any situation:

Does this need to be said?

Does this need to be said by me?

Does this need to be said by me right now?

How can I best say this?

Will I regret not speaking?

Will I regret not speaking right now?

Undoubtedly, leaders who demonstrate high emotional intelligence contribute significantly to positive outcomes on employee engagement, performance, and retention. The lack of empathy and other EQ skills significantly and negatively affect interpersonal relations at work, job performance, and employee wellbeing. Leaders who lack emotional intelligence competence are a liability to organizations. Their behavior can directly lead to employee disengagement, absenteeism, work-related stress and associated disability claims, hostile workplace lawsuits, and increased health care costs.

A key benefit of developing strong emotional intelligence skills is that you will become respected for how you lead others. You will also be respected by those you lead, even when your decisions do not align with their preferences, wants, or desires.

Emotional Intelligence and Authenticity

Emotionally self-aware leaders authentically present themselves to others and openly speak about their emotions and their efforts to manage the expression of their emotions.

Emotional intelligence is not a set of skills or tools for leaders to manipulate those they lead. This is not a situational leadership approach or a tactic to be brought forth to handle challenging circumstances or people. This is not about "messaging" or "spin." This is about leadership.

You are either authentically emotionally intelligent or you are not. Or you are on the path of becoming emotionally intelligent.

Emotionally intelligent leaders continuously and permanently monitor their words, behaviors, actions, decisions, attitudes, and mindsets.

Low emotionally intelligent leaders tend to blurt out whatever is on their minds. Their emotionally laden language is often demotivating and relationship damaging. Their mindset is about results at all costs, including human costs.

Those highly skilled in emotional intelligence are best at understanding how what they say and do affects others. They know that being congruent in their behaviors, actions, decisions, attitudes, and mindsets creates certainty and comfort for those they lead.

Being authentic is not wallowing in a "this is how I am" mindset and behavior pattern. It also does not mean sharing every thought you have with others. That is not authentic transparency and honesty. Authenticity is not an excuse or waiver for being insensitive, immature, or inappropriate.

Authentic leaders do not hide behind their mistakes, flaws, or doubts. Rather, they seek to understand these and strive to improve in the areas they can (and hire for the skills gaps they cannot close or are not inclined to fix). As we will discuss later in *Humony Leadership*, pursuing increased leadership skills is a lifelong learning quest.

Do not worry about slip-ups. You are human and are unlikely to exhibit perfect emotional intelligence 100% of the time. Perfection is not an attainable goal. And making the occasional error does not negate authenticity.

You will behave emotionally unintelligent at times. You will occasionally allow your emotions to impact decisions. You will say things you regret. You will react instead of responding to people, situations, and events. You will continue to be human.

Unlike IQ, which changes only marginally in adults, EQ can be developed, practiced, and enhanced throughout your life.

When it comes to authenticity and emotional intelligence, here are five simple questions to be asking yourself constantly:

> Can you be trusted to do what you say you will do?

> Can you be trusted to communicate openly, honestly, and transparently with sensitivity, maturity, and appropriateness?

> Are you authentically who you say and present yourself to be?

> Are your connections with those you lead (and those you interact with) authentic? Do these connections authentically matter?

> What is the most emotionally intelligent way to engage with each person or group?

Three words will make you more emotionally intelligent and authentic as a leader: I don't know.

When appropriate, admit that you do not have all the answers. Sometimes, not even all the questions. Too many leaders and managers feel pressured to make all the decisions and to do so correctly. That is not always possible.

It is hard to know when you have all the right and relevant information in your possession. People often complain about not having enough information to make a decision. Often it is the opposite – too much information to cope with and insufficient time to sift through the data to determine which information is most relevant and helpful for making a decision. Additionally, previous experience may not be relevant to today's post-pandemic world.

The reality is simple. You will face times when you will not know the most optimal solution. Admitting this to yourself and others, then welcoming help and ideas is the better path. Accepting that you need more information, different perspectives, or a team approach takes humility and confidence, two powerful traits of a Humony Leader.

Low EQ

Those with low EQ are unable to control the expressions of their emotions. This leads to unprofessional outbursts of anger, meanness, bullying, and other forms of incivility. There is no longer room for such emotional expressions in today's workplace, no matter how "passionate" a person claims to be.

Anger management and emotional regulation skills can be taught. The person who says "that's just the way I am" merely attempts to justify their behavior. One wonders, do they swear in church? Do they bully people outside work or in their families? Bullying and anger are not the only ways to produce results! People can change.

Common phrases and behaviors indicating low EQ in people include:

Lack of eye contact

I do not have time for this

I do not care

Get to the point

Multitasking or faking interest when listening

I don't trust (name)

Not replying to email

Withholding or reluctant sharing of information

Satisfaction derived from seeing others fail or make mistakes

Non-apologies: "I am sorry, but…"

Dismissing the emotions of others: "I am sorry you feel that way, but…"

Another interesting revelation from recent research is that when we are angry, we apparently believe we are smarter than everyone else around us. This tendency to instinctively think that everyone is dumber than ourselves when we are furious and feverishly angry was discovered in 2018 in a research study published in the journal *Intelligence*. The researchers studied people with trait anger.

The Encyclopedia of Behavioral Medicine defines trait anger as a "dispositional characteristic where one experiences frequent anger, with varying intensity and is often accompanied by related negative emotions such as envy, resentment, hate, and disgust."

People afflicted with trait anger are often described as having fiery personalities characterized by hot-temperateness. They are also more likely to get angry and display signs of narcissism. Not surprisingly, they believe their world revolves around them and tend to go into episodes of rage when it does not.

Those with trait anger are more likely to wrongly think they are far more intelligent than the people around them and thus less likely to consider the thoughts and ideas of others when making decisions. It is also harder to rationally argue with people with trait anger as they tend to react angrily to any comments or suggestions opposing their views.

Start With Empathy. Progress to Compassion.

Organizational leadership focus during the pandemic was often on protecting the top and bottom lines (to the best of their abilities), retaining cash flow, adapting to work-from-home mandates, and figuring out how to best protect the health and safety of employees and customers in company facilities.

Nothing wrong with that. But how many leaders also made it a strategic priority to keep morale high among employees? To understand the individual plights, anxieties, and traumas that their employees were going through? To express and exhibit compassion for the individual situations people were dealing with?

Unfortunately, far too few. Until those resignation emails started arriving, resulting in a crescendo of faux empathetic statements and expressions of "we need you, please stay." By then, it was too late and too inauthentic to have any effect.

Some are touting empathy as the #1 skill for leaders. I would not go that far, though it is definitely a highly important skill for successfully leading people. Those with empathy know how to explain ideas and strategies in ways other people understand.

They also work well with people from diverse backgrounds and cultures.

Great leadership requires a fine mix of skills to create the conditions for employee engagement, performance, and harmony. Empathy is definitely near the top of the list of what you as a leader must get right.

Empathy is the ability to notice and comprehend the observable and unspoken emotions and feelings of others. You do not need to be a psychologist to do so. Nor do you need any training in psychology, though any educational introduction to human behavior, motivation theories, or non-verbal communication is helpful. The emotions you will encounter in others most often in the workplace include uncertainty, anxiety, fear, worry, and concerns.

Empathy is a skill that can be built. It can also be faked, but that is not advisable. Authentic empathy creates greater connections and links with others. But empathy alone is not enough for leaders. You have to convert your empathy into compassion.

A study of nearly 900 employees by Catalyst found that empathy has some significant constructive effects:

> **Innovation**: When people reported their leaders were empathetic, they were more likely to report they were able to be innovative — 61% of employees compared to only 13% of employees with less empathetic leaders.

> **Engagement**: 76% of people who experienced empathy from their leaders reported they were

engaged, compared with only 32% who experienced less empathy from managers and leaders.

Retention: 57% of white women and 62% of women of color said they were unlikely to think of leaving their companies when they felt their life circumstances were respected and valued by their companies. However, when they did not feel that level of value or respect for their life circumstances, only 14% of white women and 30% of women of color said they were unlikely to consider leaving.

Inclusivity: 50% of people with empathetic leaders reported their workplace was inclusive, compared with only 17% of those with less empathetic leadership.

Work-Life: When people felt their leaders were more empathetic, 86% reported a better ability to navigate the demands of their work and life — successfully juggling their personal, family, and work obligations. This is in contrast to the 60% who perceived less empathy.

While empathy is an important skill, so too is compassion. Some leadership thinkers even place a higher value on compassion. One such thought leader, Rasmus Hougaard, founder of the Potential Project, says, "*Compared to leaders who tend toward empathy, highly compassionate leaders feel more confidence in their ability to lead others and are less likely to experience personal distress or be overwhelmed by negative emotions.*"

From a psychological viewpoint, there are three types of empathy: emotional empathy, cognitive empathy, and empathic concern (compassionate empathy).

Emotional empathy is sharing the feelings of another, such as becoming sad because someone else is sad. Cognitive empathy is understanding how someone else feels about their predicament or situation and why. Leaders are often taught this kind of empathy – rationally (but unemotionally) understanding that another is being affected by their emotional state. Empathetic concern is being motivated to help or improve another's wellbeing, particularly in the moment.

There are positives and concerns embedded in empathy and being empathetic. For instance, emotional empathy can result in absorbing too much of the emotions, issues, and challenges of others without the ability to separate ourselves from them. Cognitive empathy, on the other hand, is cerebrally understanding another's perspective without emotional resonance or understanding. This often results in emotional distance or disconnection with the other person. It can also result in seeing the other person as weak or weaker than you.

Empathy is an internal feeling. As a leader of people, your empathy needs to be converted into action. That action is compassion when the other person is in a negative emotional state. When the other person is in a positive emotional state (giddiness, glee, happy, gloating, enthusiastic, etc.), your leadership actions should be supportive and reinforcing.

Such empathetic concern combines cognitive and emotional understandings of another's perspectives or emotions coupled with advice or action without getting caught up in their issues or problems. Being strong in this type of empathy enables you to take practical action or provide viable support, whichever the other person needs.

You must set boundaries to have compassionate empathy. This is important to protect yourself, those you lead, and those with whom you engage.

Yes, it may be hard to separate yourself from the problems and challenges of your team members, especially when their pain, agony, and angst feels palpable to you. Also, it is hard to do when you are exhausted from the weight of your own issues. It is important to cultivate healthy empathy skills that do not deplete you or render you unable to lead due to empathy fatigue.

The Power of Empathetic and Compassionate Leadership

If we want people to bring their whole selves to work, we must realize that this includes their emotional and rational selves. This means they will bring both their professional emotional selves (how they feel about the workplace environment, their jobs, and their colleagues) and their personal emotional selves (anything and everything impacting them outside work). Thus, leaders need to know everything happening in society and the local community that might be impacting their employees.

And this is not easy, particularly when you are remotely leading individuals and teams or if your socio-economic conditions differ significantly from those you lead. In such situations, having empathy and showing compassion requires extra, concentrated effort.

Today, our world seems fixated on what divides people, societies, communities, and nations. Powerful forces, including politicians, religious leaders, and the media, are tearing everyone apart. As a result, a good portion of the population in many countries is embracing and openly expressing anger in public and in workplaces. People are boiling and seething. And, as they actively reject empathy for those with whom they disagree, their discordant attitudes and behaviors permeate workplaces across the globe.

In this environment, having empathy and expressing compassion is the radical act that leaders need to display. You must nip frictional behavior, words, and actions in the bud. Do not allow these to spread. You have to take a hard stand and put an end to anything incompatible with workplace harmony.

We may not be able to fix all the issues dividing people today, but as leaders we can certainly learn (or relearn) how to show compassion and assist people affected by internal and societal events.

And if you think that showing empathy and expressing compassion will make you look weak as a leader, research shows otherwise. Numerous academic studies have confirmed that empathic individuals excel professionally. Even better, they also experience higher levels of wellbeing.

Other research has proven that the most successful workplace teams are those in which employees report high levels of psychological safety and interpersonal sensitivity. Studies have also shown that those who are empathetic are prone to be seen by their peers as natural leaders. They are also most likely to rise through the ranks via regular promotions.

Hence, throw out the notion that kindness, empathy, and compassion are incompatible with success. Gone are the days when a hard-nosed, unemotional approach to people leadership is the only path to organizational and personal success. Such thinking is outdated and diametrically opposite to long-term, sustainable success in today's world. Empathetic and compassionate leadership is the more fruitful path to take.

Sadly, many leaders subdue their empathetic skills as they gain more executive power, probably because their bonuses and stock options are linked solely to financial and operational results. Do not let this happen to you.

And when you get into a position within your organization to change this inferior mindset, do so. Make empathetic and compassionate leadership the yardstick for organizational success (in conjunction with financial and operational results).

By developing strong emotional intelligence skills and competencies, you will become more effective at leading others – and yourself – even in times of uncertainty, ambiguity, and change.

As a result, you will be highly sought after for leadership positions within your current organization and outside entities. There may be no single more important factor for a successful leadership career trajectory than proficiency in emotional intelligence.

As such, emotional intelligence is a cornerstone skill for Humony Leaders.

When we can free ourselves
from the idea of separateness,
we have compassion, we have understanding,
and we have the energy we need to help.
Thich Nhat Hanh

CHAPTER 5

Dealing With Uncertainty and Ambiguity

The future will reward clarity but it will punish certainty.
Dr. Bob Johansen
Institute for the Future

O ne of the most important leadership skills today is navigating uncertainty. That means knowing what you can control and what you cannot, what you can and cannot predict, and planning for an uncertain, ambiguous, and frequently changing future.

While it is trite to say that the only constant is change, that phrase has never been a more accurate description of our world. Not only has the pace of change quickened, it now arrives from various angles: artificial intelligence, rapidly spreading global viruses, governments closing borders, societal disruptions, changing attitudes about work and workplace environments, supply chain issues, and the disintegration of social cohesion.

Call it a tsunami of change. Or a trembling earthquake of disruption and destruction. Or a tidal wave of erosion bringing forth new ways of thinking and interactions. However you choose to label or describe it, massive change is upon us and will be with us for the foreseeable future.

Uncertainty arises when important and relevant information is unavailable, combined with not knowing if or how short-term changes will evolve into long-term trends (such as the desire for many workers for hybrid or complete working-from-home situations).

The initial reaction to uncertainty and ambiguity is normally defensive. The immediate, reactionary attention of senior leaders and business owners is often to protect cash flow by cutting marketing and training budgets. Next is to freeze hiring while simultaneously figuring out how to protect the client base. Then comes the reflexive and impulsive "reduction in force" maneuver to lower headcount and salary costs.

Such defensive moves are the common reactions to large-scale uncertainty, as we saw at the beginning of the pandemic. But they can be counterproductive, especially for the long term. Two examples illustrate this.

First, despite billions in government aid, the airline industry in the United States furloughed thousands of workers in the early days of the pandemic. Eighteen months later, when the travel market was starting to rebound, these same airlines canceled thousands of flights during the peak holiday traffic period in 2021 due to insufficient staff. Unfortunately, these staffing issues have continued into the 2022 summer holiday season (a sure sign that the industry remains plagued by managerial mindsets).

Second, several research studies confirmed that the lack of development, training, and opportunities for growth during coronavirus lockdowns, due to the obliteration of corporate training and development programs, was a central factor causing millions to join the Great Resignation of 2021-22.

In both examples, decisions by leaders to react – instead of to respond – to the uncertainty surrounding the pandemic have slowed the rebound coming out of the pandemic. These decisions have also dramatically increased the workloads and stress levels for remaining employees, thus creating other problems to be dealt with down the road.

Today's Environment

We are operating today in a real-time laboratory best called the New Abnormal.

Go back a year ago (from late February 2022 as this is being written). How likely would you have predicted 7% to 8% annual inflation rates in the U.S. and other major economies, the Russian invasion of Ukraine, the Omicron strain of coronavirus, or the airline industry canceling thousands of flights during the peak holiday season of 2021 due to insufficient staffing?

In 2019, a pre-pandemic study of global business leaders identified comfort with risk and ambiguity as the top skills required for leaders. Post-pandemic 2022 and beyond, the need for these leadership skills has been amplified.

The absence of clarity and certainty defines today's New Abnormal laboratory for leaders in businesses, governments, non-profit organizations, and every other entity that exists. The best leaders will be those able to live with ambiguity with a comfort level and sense of humility that others will be unable to muster.

The leaders who become best at leading through uncertainty will rely heavily on diverse inputs and collaborative teamwork. Such leaders know – or will learn – that they alone are unlikely to have the combination of skills, knowledge, experiences, or perspectives for crafting optimal solutions or strategies. Unilateral decision making is no longer a characteristic of smart or great leaders.

Instead, successful leaders will assemble teams that can collaborate cooperatively. They will then trust these teams to compile the information, ideas, and options needed to thrive in an uncertain world. Then together, the leaders and the teams can weigh, analyze, and choose between the available options and the permutations of each when (not if) circumstances change.

Our Brains Are Not Built to Handle Uncertainty

Unfortunately, our brains are not designed to cope effortlessly with ambiguity and uncertainty.

Our brains are remarkably proficient at recognizing patterns. This enables us to build solid habits and perform numerous tasks (getting dressed, driving, eating, showering, etc.) on autopilot. This makes us highly efficient creatures, as long as the status quo remains relatively stable and constant.

However, such efficiency goes out the door when massive change or unfamiliar situations crop up. When things are happening outside recognizable patterns, our brains have difficulty coping. In fact, they tend to seize on anything remotely familiar or recognizable. If none exist, our uncertainty-adverse brains rapidly go into a risk-averse mode (known as the fight-flight-freeze mode).

Understandably, this impacts decision making. It also can affect confidence, focus, motivation, self-control, and overall wellbeing. It can even impact the willingness to cooperate with others, unless such cooperation is viewed as related to self-preservation.

Unfortunately, being human beings, leaders are not wired to cope with uncertainty easily. As humans, we seek certainty. Our brains are wired to look for patterns and build habits as a survival mechanism. That makes us ill-disposed to uncertainty and ambiguous situations. When numerous sources of uncertainty occur simultaneously, or in response to one another, feelings of being overwhelmed are added into the mix.

This exacerbating stew combining external chaos, emotional hijackings, and downbeat internal dialogues is not a good recipe for optimum decision making when facing uncertainty or ambiguity. And like the pandemic virus, this easily cascades from one person to another, especially within tightly knit groups like leadership teams. Yet, it is precisely in these conditions that so many decisions are made, with far-reaching consequences impacting hundreds or even thousands.

Feelings of uncertainty, especially if overwhelming, shift the brain into survival mode. Uncertainty and ambiguity are seen as a threat. As discussed earlier, one aspect of this is a tendency of the brain to resort to binary decision making, where the brain limits our choices to only two options (A or B, black or white, this or that, etc.). In such a state, the brain cannot contemplate, or cope with, multiple ideas, options, or choices. It also reduces our access to long-term memory and even decreases working memory availability.

Fortunately, we can manage our brains with concentrated effort, rather than permitting our brains to manage us. Four of the best ways to get control of the brain's autonomic reactions to ambiguity and uncertainty are:

1) focus on realistic expectations

2) maintain a modicum of genuine and authentic optimism

3) focus on big-picture goals and long-term objectives

4) be candid with yourself and others about the level of uncertainty and ambiguity being encountered

Leading Through Uncertainty

Navigating uncertainty and ambiguity is a critical business and leadership skill. One that is at a premium in today's market for leaders and managers. Doing so means knowing what you can and cannot control or influence.

It also requires aligning your team to a shared and preferred outcome, which focuses on progress rather than stated objectives. After all, objectives and goals are often best guesses on achievable results. Accuracy has never been a core component of results forecasting (actual results are almost always either above or below the stipulated projections, for targets are rarely hit exactly 100% as planned or forecasted).

Leaders must learn how to develop a suitable mindset to excel at adapting and dealing with uncertainty and ambiguity. Encountering and handling ambiguity and uncertainty should be seen as a highly marketable job skill called Leading in Uncertainty. I would ask any job candidate for a leadership position this insightful question: "give me an example of when you had to make a decision or create a plan in a situation where all the facts were not at hand and the future uncertain."

The follow-up question would be, "what did you learn about yourself, your team, and leading your team from this?" Note that this follow-up question focuses on what they learned from their experience, not what results or outcomes were generated. Lessons learned can be replicated. Outcomes and results are situational.

At the core of this mindset is having an open mind. Start with a willingness to question your assumptions and predictions about the future. Are you merely extrapolating the past or present into the future? Do you tend to see abrupt changes as short-term hurdles that will recede once you have adapted to them? Do you long for a past normalcy, or are you excited about an unpredictable future?

Having an open mind means being receptive to the thoughts, ideas, suggestions, and recommendations of others. Being receptive does not equate to acceptance of the notions, opinions, and positions of others. The best leadership practice is to mix and combine these inputs with your perspective, experience, and knowledge base. Doing so ignites the flames of innovation, creativity, and better decision making.

Utilizing an open mind is done best with humility and humbleness. This requires recognizing that you do not have all the answers (and sometimes not even all of the most relevant and pertinent questions). Accept that your ideas, concepts, strategies, and plans may have missing components or unknown weaknesses. Be appreciative and grateful when others point out or help you identify these gaps and drawbacks in your thinking.

Success rarely comes strictly from others executing your ideas. Rather, success comes from working together, building upon each other's experiences, knowledge, ideas, insights, and perspectives. Especially when aiming to make progress despite surrounding uncertainty and ambiguity.

Remember, everyone seeks certainty. How can you provide certainty to your team members and colleagues during periods of high uncertainty?

The answer is to be open with your communications. Be willing to share the framework of your decision-making process. Tell your team members: "we do not have all the answers at this time. So here is what we will do in the interim. And here is how we will work together to determine the most optimal solutions based on the best information we can gather."

This creates time and conditions for you and your team members to figure out an optimal solution. Or for them to entrust you and your co-leaders to do so. If the latter, it is critical to keep your team members constantly informed of any changes, externally or internally, that are likely to impact your thinking.

Doing so cultivates trust and confidence with your team members while simultaneously helping reduce their individual and collective stresses and anxieties stemming from uncertainty and unknowing. This also helps prevent the rampant spread of unfounded rumors from spreading, something that would escalate the stress and anxiety for many.

In effect, this openness with your team members becomes the very anchor of certainty for them (providing you deliver diligently upon all your promises to them).

This practice also helps to de-escalate ambiguity and uncertainty by accepting and turning these into new norms. Not just a new normality, however. A new norm that you, your fellow leaders, and your team members are capable of coping with and mastering.

Interestingly, it is human nature to forecast the future mainly by extrapolating recent events and experiences, albeit sometimes with slight alterations, unendingly into the foreseeable future. This is dangerous even in relatively stable times. In exceedingly uncertain times, like the present, this is simply madness.

It is also human nature to become unmoored – helplessly awash at sea, so to speak – when these extrapolated and deduced futures are rudely interrupted by a cascade of changing circumstances and conditions. Our anxiety levels escalate when we realize that our expectations are unlikely to materialize in the manner we foresaw. Additionally, our decisions become influenced more by turbulent emotions than steady, rational thoughts. And we tend to react in ways that are not ideal or even constructive.

Understanding these human tendencies enables Humony Leaders to know themselves and recognize their decision-making limitations. They also learn to comprehend and appreciate how disrupted change and uncertain futures impact their team members.

This is why openly communicating with your staff and involving them in identifying problem-solving options are best practices in minimizing the disturbances caused by the intrusion of uncertainty and ambiguity.

Periods of volatility and instability are not the time for faux positivity and artificial motivational speeches. Neither deception nor blind optimism should be considered. These times call for truth, honesty, and humbly admitting that not all the answers are immediately at hand.

Additionally, if you are not open and transparent in your communications, you prevent your team members and others from planning and acting upon reality and currently known data.

Your role in leading through uncertainty and ambiguity is orchestrating ideas, thoughts, and decisions while concurrently harmonizing a positive atmosphere within your team and quelling the rise of stress and anxiety through open and transparent communications. This means helping your team members grapple with their own emotions and concerns and facilitating their confidence that they and you will find successful ways to embark into the immediate future despite all the uncertainty and ambiguity you face.

This leadership behavior determines whether your team members respond to uncertainty and ambiguity with creativity and productivity, or whether they react by becoming overstressed, demotivated, withdrawn, or resigned to helplessness. In short, a leader's ability to continuously create an environment enabling everyone to excel at handling uncertainty and ambiguity will determine the success level the team can achieve in today's fluid world of constant change and unpredictability.

Mistakes can cause us to feel vulnerable and uncertain. Again, a leadership mindset change is required, one that needs to be openly discussed and practiced within every team. This mental attitude is that mistakes and judgment errors will happen, especially in times of uncertainty and ambiguity. Part of resiliency (see next chapter) is about turning these mistakes into lessons that decrease the feeling of vulnerability and increase the skills of coping with uncertainty.

How? By embracing uncertainty. As Janice Marturano, founder and executive director of the Institute for Mindful Leadership, says, "*We are not talking about the uncertainty disappearing. We are talking about turning toward it and using our principles to help us guide how we act in the moment. We cannot change everything around us, but we can change how we meet it.*"

Uncertainty and ambiguity will never disappear. Mastering ambiguity and uncertainty starts with accepting these and turning into them, not away from them. You have to create principles around methods for handling ambiguity and certainty through your mental outlook, the questions you ask, the data you seek, and how to plan for contingencies and possibilities. These principles will guide you in periods of uncertainty and ambiguity and when situations become clearer and less vague.

Tips for Leading Through Uncertainty

You do not have to like dealing with uncertainty and ambiguity to be good at this skill. You simply need to start by reducing your uncomfortableness with ambiguity and uncertainty.

Note that I say reducing – not eliminating – being uncomfortable with ambiguity and uncertainty. A modicum level of uncomfortableness is good. After all, we do not grow as individuals, teams, or organizations without getting out of our comfort zones. We only get better when we move from our comfort zone into the growth zone.

For instance, one does not become an accomplished snowboarder by staying on the introductory bunny slopes. No, to become a good snowboarder, you must gradually conquer new slopes and hills, all of which will initially be outside your comfort zone.

One of the best ways to lead through uncertainty is by continuously upskilling yourself and your team members. Numerous studies also show that upskilling programs have a positive impact on retaining and attracting talent, as well as on productivity.

One thing the pandemic highlighted is the tremendous mismatch between the incumbent skills of the workforce (and of leaders) and the skills required for future success. Leading remotely, for instance, became an immediate skill need in March and April 2020. Now, hiring and onboarding remotely are requisite skills.

Additionally, many research studies show a direct and measurable connection between upskilling staff and employee engagement. For example, the PwC 2020 Global Digital IQ survey revealed that 86% of respondents agreed that their digital training and education programs had improved employee engagement and performance. With Gallup reporting a 17% increase in productivity and a 41% reduction in absenteeism in highly engaged business units, the multiplier effect of upskilling is evident.

Rather than hiring for new talent, with all the uncertainties and ambiguities that this entails, upskilling of current staff (and contract workers) needs to be a priority in a world where the speed and continuation of change are unparalleled and the future is framed with ambiguity and uncertainty. The employees remaining with you post-pandemic and despite the Great Resignation trends since the middle of 2021 have proven their loyalty and capabilities to move your organization forward in a wildly uncertain period.

As mentioned previously, the lack of development opportunities has been cited in several research studies as a key factor in the Great Resignation. That is not surprising. Workers are aware of and admittedly concerned about their skill gaps. In a 2021 study by PwC of over 32,000 workers around the globe, more than 75% said they want to improve their skills. Another global study, by software company UiPath, of 4500 office workers worldwide revealed that 88% would be more willing to continue working for an organization that offered upskilling and reskilling opportunities.

Continuous upskilling of leaders, managers, supervisors, and individual contributors creates a growth mindset culture within an organization. It also increases confidence in individuals and teams that they are better prepared to handle an uncertain future. Later in this book, I will highlight other benefits of a lifelong learning mindset.

Create Trust Not Certainty

Build trust by understanding and accepting that mistakes and errors in judgment will be made by your team members, colleagues, peers, and yourself.

Those who thrive in uncertain and volatile external and internal environments will be those able to adjust and adapt to ambiguity and uncertainty. They will see mistakes, setbacks, and failures as part of their growth evolution. They will learn from these miscues and march forth successfully with these lessons and experiences firmly in hand.

You may not be able to control or impact the changes happening to you, your team, and your organization. But you can become better prepared to change how you meet, handle, and even leverage the changes that arrive.

Lastly, do not be afraid to use periods of ambiguity to try something new. Experiment! And learn from the successes or iterations of your experiments.

We do not fear the unknown.
We fear what we think we know
about the unknown.
Teal Swan

CHAPTER 6

Resilience

It is how you deal with failure that determines
how you achieve success.
David Feherty

Closely aligned to handling ambiguity and uncertainty is resilience.

A resilient person is one who rebounds and recovers quickly from difficult situations or setbacks. You stop negative momentum dead in its tracks when you can do this in your professional and personal lives. Resiliency is a skill enabling someone to respond to any situation in a way that helps them progress to their desired future self.

Much like grit and fortitude, resilience is a skill developed through facing difficult times, moving through them, and learning from the experience. Just as you cannot learn to swim without getting into the water, you cannot develop and hone your resilience muscles without facing up to challenges, difficulties, disappointments, and setbacks.

You grow resilience by tapping into a positive mindset and being convinced that the troubles and problems of today are providing lessons that will benefit you in the future.

This open, growth mindset enables resilient people to become flexible, adaptable, and agile when encountering future hurdles, obstacles, letdowns, frustrations, and failures.

Resilience also enables you to get past stoppages, blocks, barriers, and impediments when pursuing a task or goal. Strong resilience provides an intrinsic desire to continue, endure, and push past inclinations to procrastinate or quit.

Resilient people create resilient organizations. That is an important concept for leaders to recognize. The leader cannot be the only resilient person on the team.

While leaders must exhibit and exude resiliency, they must also coach and teach resilience skills to their team members. Like the truth in the idiom "one bad apple spoils the barrel," it only takes one non-resilient person to spoil or undercut a team's ability in this area.

Resilient teams are designed for adaptability and flexibility. They are capable of quickly changing course when necessary. But this can happen only when the team comprises individuals with strong resilience skills and acute confidence in themselves and others on the team. Resilient organizations that are agile will be powerful organizations for years to come.

Some people confuse resiliency with tenacity. Tenacity is more about staying the course and holding on despite obstacles. Resilience is the ability to bounce back from setbacks, combined with the willingness to alter course, when necessary, without blame association or guilt. (The skill of tenacity will be discussed in chapter eight.)

Resilience starts in the mind and how you manage your thoughts. The brain's plasticity enables us to be resilient during challenging times. We can learn how to calm down, reassess and reframe situations, refocus our thoughts, and teach ourselves to respond and not react to people, situations, and events.

In fact, the most powerful way to fight and manage stress is to consistently work on building your mental strength, resilience strategies, and coping mechanisms.

Preparing to weather future crises and the ongoing world of uncertainty and ambiguity will require a flexible, knowledgeable workforce and work environment built on resilience.

Building Resiliency

The American Psychological Association defines resilience as "the process of adapting well in the face of adversity, trauma, tragedy, threats, or significant sources of stress."

This definition applies equally to teams as individuals.

Have you ever thought about your relationship with resilience? In today's times, you should:

Is resiliency one of your strong suits?

How can you build stronger resiliency, both professionally and personally?

As Linda Graham wrote, "*Resilience is essential to the survival and thriving of human beings.*"

Dr. Martin Seligman and his team at the University of Pennsylvania developed the PERMA model, which outlines the five pillars for flourishing and thriving at work and beyond.

These are the five key factors they identified that contribute to positive wellbeing:

Positive emotions

Engagement

Relationships

Meaning

Accomplishment

I would suggest that these are also five critical contributors to resiliency as well. Each is a factor upon which resiliency can be built and maintained. Plus, in today's world, it is difficult to flourish and thrive without strong resiliency skills.

We grow emotional and mental resilience when we tap into self-confidence, have a positive mindset, and apply the lessons from previous hindrances, dissatisfactions, and disillusionments to current circumstances and situations. In doing so, we increase and enhance our resiliency skills, positioning us for greater and continued success in the future.

If you think of emotions as energy in motion, then the importance of growing emotional resilience is clear. As explained earlier in chapter four, knowing what triggers your emotions and then being equipped to manage the expression of these emotions are true signs of emotional intelligence. Emotional resiliency is bouncing back from the occasions when you do not or cannot control how your emotions get expressed or how you allow your emotions to impact your attitude, decisions, or mental wellbeing.

The best way to put the energy of your emotions in the right direction is through a daily practice of positive thinking. I am not suggesting putting on rose-colored glasses or singing Bob Marley's *Don't Worry Be Happy* song every morning. Research shows, however, that focusing on the things going right in your world is better for you emotionally than dwelling on the negatives, no matter how deeply impacting or alarming are the adverse events or situations you are facing.

A key to this is recalling previous instances of undesirable circumstances and how you got through those situations. We all have periods of downbeat moods and pessimistic thoughts. Yet we get past those moments unless we slip into despair or depression. In which case, professional assistance is the recommended course of action.

Fortunately, a daily practice of positive thinking can help prevent falling down a slippery slope into desolation, hopelessness, or despondency.

Resiliency, of course, is a dynamic process and skill. It is not a fixed human characteristic or attribute. The bad news is that resiliency ebbs and flows in each of us. The good news is that it is a skill and attribute that can be built, grown, and leveraged.

Remember, for happiness and joy to be truly appreciated, we must experience and endure periods of darkness. Building resiliency often results from combining positivity with a renewed focus on purpose. Ask yourself:

> *How can you serve others? At work? In your personal life? In your community?*
>
> *How can you ensure your physical, mental, and*

emotional cups are full? What energizes you? Why? How can you incorporate these energizers into your daily life?

What brings you joy? Why? How can you include joy-inspiring elements or items into your daily life? If not daily, how about every other day?

Where are the opportunities for you to show kindness to others? At work? In your home or personal life? In social interactions with strangers?

Where are the opportunities for you to exhibit compassion to others? At work? In your personal or home life? In social interactions with strangers?

It is often said that humans are social creatures craving the company of and interaction with others. For some, such as the highly introverted, this is less true than for others. However, at the very roots of being human, we derive immense self-satisfaction and pleasure from helping others and being kind to others when not forced to do so by social niceties or constraints.

So, when things are going tough. Or you have had a recent failure or setback. And when things are not working out exactly the way you had anticipated or hoped, one of the best ways to develop resiliency is by helping others or being kind and compassionate to those not in a position to repay your humanist deeds. That is fine. The true rewards for such acts come in the glow of self-satisfaction and the associated feeling of being a kind and worthy human being.

Centering your thoughts on the positive and rewarding emotions stemming from these actions helps build your resiliency muscles. Here are a dozen steps to become more resilient:

1. Accept change – it is guaranteed to continue to happen.

2. Become comfortable with change – find ways to become calmer and more contented with change, knowing you can thrive during change.

3. Reframe – shift how you view your mindsets, attitudes, skills, and talents.

4. Drop blame – be future focused. Blame is for the past. Understand the lessons and prepare for the future.

5. Convert your thinking – do not ask, "why is this happening to me?" Ask instead, "what can I learn from this?"

6. Be a continuous learner – always be learning new skills and techniques and prepare to apply them in periods of change.

7. Reflect – introspection fosters learning, unearths new perspectives, and hones self-awareness.

8. Take ownership of your career – take charge of your personal and professional development. You have personal accountability for this.

9. Know your sense of purpose – knowing your personal North Star helps position setbacks within a broader and more important perspective framework.

10. Reframe self-identity – formulate your identity apart from your job, based on the whole you, not just the professional you.

11. Cultivate relationships – develop and nurture a

broad network of personal and professional relationships.

12. Personal interests – pursue hobbies and interests outside the workplace.

Resiliency in Practice

What does this mean for you as a leader? For one, you do not want your negative mood, no matter how temporary, to affect the people you lead. Team members are extremely good at knowing when the boss is in an unpleasant or bad mood. They are also excellent at discerning when their leader is pessimistic, unconfident, negative, or cynical.

So, when you are having a bad day, focus your attention on how you can help or coach your team members. Concentrate on building their skills and knowledge rather than on your gloomy thoughts. Give your attention to their needs instead of a single-minded rumination on what is not going according to plan.

This may seem like an awkward or strange approach. After all, if something has gone astray or if you have made an error, shouldn't you be giving this your full attention? No, not if your brain is awash in a negative emotional state. Solutions rarely arise from a negative mental framework. Solutions require contemplating options, choices, multiple "what if" scenarios, and the positive mental chatter that a solution will be found.

Thus, instead of tackling a problem or trying to recover from a setback with a head full of anguish and self-criticism, put that mindset aside and give your attention to helping others.

Then, when serotonin, dopamine, endorphins, and oxytocin – the four so-called happy chemicals of the brain – kick in, you will be in a better mental and emotional state for creating a resolution, or a new plan of action, to overcome and surmount the problem or situation you are facing. With this methodology, problems and circumstances that appear overwhelming soon become transitory and short-lived.

The other advantage of this process is that you will become fully present and more effective as a people leader. Additionally, you will make better decisions while strengthening your capability to rebound quicker from future setbacks.

The other important aspect of resiliency is to be tolerant of the mistakes by yourself and others. Learning and growth come from making mistakes. Think of such errors as part of the iterative process, not failures. People grow, individually and collectively, by learning from mistakes and determining solutions for their slipups, including their errors of misjudgment and poor decision making.

Perfection rarely happens. Accept that. Also, accept that what has worked previously might no longer be the most viable approach for today. The world has changed. Situations have changed. Wonderfully created solutions of the past may need to evolve over time. For instance, the U.S. Constitution has been modified with 27 amendments to date.

As I wrote at the start of this chapter, resilient people create resilient organizations. One key role of a leader is to build resilience in themselves and their team members. Doing so will enable you and your team to handle uncertainty and ambiguity better and place you and the team in a better position to take corrective action to turn circumstances, mistakes, and errors into temporary and impermanent setbacks.

A proven method for building resiliency within your team is to share your own stories of how and when you rebounded from a setback. For instance, how did you overcome a time when your manager did not accept your ideas or recommendations, especially early in your career? How have you handled change situations in the past, particularly when you were not completely bought into the change?

Or, share a time that you did not succeed at something. How did you handle it? How did you course correct? And most importantly, what did you learn about yourself from this incident?

Remember, the most important lessons from setbacks are not the solutions derived for fixing the situation but what the person learns about themselves and their capacity for being resilient. So, in the latter example, do not focus on the business or personal solution lesson but on what it taught you about yourself and your resilience capabilities.

Once you have set the stage for this openness, encourage other team members to share their resiliency stories and lessons. This may take a while, so be patient. A few one-on-one conversations with some team members might prompt them to be more open and sharing, especially if you tell them how doing so will showcase their personal leadership skills to you and the rest of the team.

Often, people think resiliency just means pushing through and working harder. Again, this is more tenacity than resiliency, though people do attempt to bounce back through greater focus, effort, and work. Unfortunately, this typically leads to overexertion, which in turn cascades into mental and physical burnout.

Hard work and increased effort, up to a point, can be beneficial. But without the right mental state and self-care routine, simply working harder and longer hours is likely to do more harm than good.

Also, do not be afraid to inject some fun into your workplace climate. Fun is known to boost human resilience and spirits in ways that make it easier to cope with whatever life (and work) throws your way. The state of flow that comes from having fun, laughing, and enjoyment lowers stress and enhances emotional, mental, and physical health.

Getting the brain to focus on funny and joyful things can help to counteract the tendency of the brain to concentrate on negative thoughts and constantly scan for threats, which keeps the brain locked into a cycle of negativity. Plus, when we are having fun, we are more authentic, let down our guard, and enjoy the companionship of others in a lighthearted manner.

Building a Resilience Mindset

A place to start building personal resiliency is your mindset about the future. Are your thoughts optimistic or pessimistic? Why?

There is a strong symbiotic relationship between being positive and resilience. Research by Barbara Fredrickson, a psychological researcher at the University of North Carolina at Chapel Hill, has shown that positivity and resiliency are each important for the other. For instance, being in a positive mood makes people more resilient physically.

Additionally, a major finding from her studies is that resilient people take a different attitude toward difficult or fearful tasks (such as giving a presentation) than non-resilient individuals. They view such tasks as challenges and opportunities for growth rather than threats or chances to fail.

Resilient people do not delude themselves with false or self-manifested feelings of positivity. Rather, they tend to let go of negative thoughts, worry less about undesirable outcomes, and can shift the focus of their attention to positive thoughts quickly and relatively easily.

Here are some ways to reframe your mindset when feeling overwhelmed:

> There is no way I will get all this done. >>> I can accomplish this one step at a time.
>
> I do not know where to begin. >>> I have prioritized successfully before and I can do so again.
>
> I am not qualified to do this work. >>> I am smart and capable, and there are resources available that I can find if necessary.

Those with high levels of resiliency report the same anxiety levels as less resilient people. However, they also report higher levels of happiness, interest, and enthusiasm for seeking solutions to problems. In such people, like all of us, positive emotions reside in unison with negative emotions. The difference is in which range of emotions and thoughts they choose to create their emotional states.

Resiliency is more about how you recharge than how you endure difficult situations. You cannot persevere for long without caring for your mental, emotional, and physical wellbeing. Sacrificing sleep to put more effort into an important project works only for the short term. Continuously doing so project after project after project is neither smart nor healthy.

The better approach is to exert yourself for a while, then take a break to recharge and re-energize before returning to a heightened effort level. Pushing yourself too hard or too long knocks your system out of balance.

When this happens, your body and brain are knocked out of alignment from overworking. You will need to expend enormous mental and physical resources returning to balance before you can move forward. Incorporating frequent periods of rest, or turning your attention to doing something pleasurable, will increase productivity, creativity, and solution generation much better and faster than stubbornly pushing on when you are mentally or physically exhausted.

Staying too long in high-performance mode results in diminishing returns. It also results in lengthier recovery periods and significantly increased risks of burnout. Additionally, rest and recovery are not the same things. We can be physically at rest, yet our minds continue battling with work matters and problem solving.

The brain needs a break just as much, sometimes more, than the body. Switching the brain away from work tasks and issues is an important component of a recovery period.

This is why taking breaks during the workday is equally important as those taken outside the work environment. Perhaps this is even more important in work-from-home situations where the boundaries, both mental and physical, between work and personal lives are heavily blurred.

Since resiliency fluctuates, you need to do regular check-ins with yourself.

Then, as a leader, you need to apply this same process to those you lead. Learn to identify when your team members, colleagues, peers, or bosses need additional resiliency support. Remember, resiliency is a dynamic process grounded in emotional stability. Hence, whenever someone's emotional stability starts to appear out of kilter, our responsibility as leaders is to lend the support they need to return to emotional equilibrium.

Mindfulness Practices Build Resilience

Another technique to build resilience is mindfulness. Mindfulness is the ability to be fully present and focused in a moment, paying particular attention to the signals of your body, mind, and emotions in a non-judgmental state. Mindfulness is the polar opposite of being in a *mind full* mode.

While mindfulness may sound like some kind of a New Age fad, it is actually a leadership skill that goes back several decades. Pierre Wack, head of Group Planning at Royal Dutch Shell in the 1970s and the famed creator of scenario planning, said that planning well required "training the mind." Mindfulness is a choice of how you want to live, both professionally and personally.

For leaders, mindfulness is not just about improving the ability to have greater control over your thoughts. It is also important and beneficial for greatly reducing the control your unconscious and habitual thoughts have over your actions and emotions.

You are going to have thoughts and emotions anyway. It is just a matter of whether you, your thoughts, or your emotions will be in control.

To regain control over your thoughts and emotions, it is necessary to disengage the autopilot mode within which so many leaders operate. Yes, working on autopilot does seem to be highly effective and productive. However, similar to the belief that multitasking is an efficient methodology for accomplishing a lot, both methods sacrifice quality for quantity and can harm interpersonal relationships and optimal decision making.

Mindfulness is an effective tool to help you navigate expectations and relationships as you maneuver toward the results you want. Equally as important, however, is that mindfulness also helps you understand and accept outcomes when you do not get what you want or desire.

Mindfulness brings into play two critical components of leadership success: intention and presence. As a leader, you are a leader of people. As Rear Admiral Grace Murray Hopper said, "*You manage things. You lead people.*" To succeed in leading people, you must be well-grounded in both your intentions and presence.

When grounded in your intentions and fully present in the moment, you are best positioned to call upon your resiliency skills. Additionally, research studies have shown that utilizing mindfulness in the workplace enhances physical and mental health, leading to improved job performance and stronger collaborative relationships.

Those who routinely use mindfulness techniques at work are typically happier, more productive, and less likely to depart to another organization or even take sick leave. They are also more likely to build stronger workplace relationships and less likely to escalate conflict as they tend to respond, not react, to people, situations, and events.

Leaders who employ mindfulness habits and techniques at work also tend to be more satisfied with their jobs, perform better than peers, and are less prone to stress-induced illnesses, mental exhaustion, and work-related burnout.

Perhaps this is why meditation – a core conduit, but not a prerequisite, to mindfulness – is practiced by thousands of corporate leaders around the world.

Workplace implementation of mindfulness is not limited to just the C-suites, either. Aetna has fully incorporated mindfulness into its corporate culture, including creating the position of a Chief Mindfulness Officer. According to an article in *Healthy Workplace*, Aetna's corporate-wide mindfulness program participants are "regaining 62 minutes per week of productivity." That is approximately $3000 per person per annum in productivity gains for the insurance giant.

Return to Purpose

Purpose drives behaviors and directs thoughts. It also stimulates self-motivation.

So, you made a mistake. Blew the budget. Anticipated the wrong outcome. Ran into an unexpected obstacle. Failed to deliver a project on time. Hired (or fired) the wrong person. Made and implemented a decision that backfired with staff or customers. These things happen to leaders across the world a thousand times a day. While that may not be a comforting thought in the moment that a negative situation is happening to you, it does help to put your particular situation into perspective. Setbacks are rarely fatal to companies or careers.

And the perspective you want to focus on is the big picture. Instead of asking, "why is this happening to me?" ask, "what is this situation trying to teach me?" And then use this answer to figure out how to realign with your personal purpose or company objective.

People with a strong sense of purpose tend to be more resilient and better able to recover from negative events and circumstances quickly. Turning your focus to a deeply rooted purpose, whether this is your individual passion or an organizational mission, boosts a desire to rebound swiftly and "get back in the saddle." Making the decision not to allow a setback to stop the pursuit of an individual or collective aspiration reignites the energy to re-engage and redouble efforts, this time with the new knowledge gained from the setback.

Great leaders know that this not only applies to them but also to their team members. A study from McKinsey concluded that "purpose can be an important contributor to employee experience, which in turn is linked to higher levels of employee engagement, stronger organizational commitment, and increased feelings of wellbeing."

Unfortunately, workplaces and jobs are no longer providing meaningful purpose for millions of people. A study from the Pew Research Center showed that the percentage of Americans deriving meaning in their lives from work had fallen from 24% in 2017 to 17% in November 2021.

Work, careers, and occupation continue to reduce as primary factors as many people rethink and reappraise what provides meaning in their lives and makes them thrive. Against this backdrop, the McKinsey researchers advise that leaders "should pay more attention to individual purpose as companies return to operations and begin feeling their way into the subsequent phases of the next normal."

As the McKinsey report states, "creating strong links to an individual purpose benefits individuals and companies alike – and could be vital in managing the post-pandemic uncertainties that lie ahead."

Those uncertainties will be handled best by individuals and teams with strong resiliency muscles as they are more likely to use curiosity to explore solutions and take action knowing they can manage and overcome future obstacles that crop up.

Focusing on purpose augments resiliency, the ability to handle ambiguity and uncertainty, and even wellbeing. Several research studies support the notion that people who live their purpose – at work and elsewhere – have up to five times higher well-being levels than those who do not. Other research also concludes that those with an elevated sense of purpose live longer and healthier lives.

Remember, it is not what happens to you that defines you; it is what you do next. A best practice is to ensure resilience is one of the elements that defines the future you.

The opportunity to develop resilience comes through difficult circumstances that both highlight and challenge existing mindsets.
Devra Davis

CHAPTER 7

Adaptability

It is not the strongest of the species that survives,
nor the most intelligent that survives.
It is the one that is most adaptable to change.
Charles Darwin

Change is certain. As an earlier chapter shows, dealing with ambiguity and uncertainty is also inevitable.

Without a doubt, the pandemic fast-tracked the importance of agility and adaptability as critical leadership and organizational skills. The next challenge for leaders is accelerating a transition to organizational designs and team construction that enables flexibility and adaptation.

Prior to the pandemic, agility was often promoted as the fast adaptation to changing circumstances. Of course, that is reactionary thinking. Leaders must now prepare to respond to uncertainty and changing circumstances by instilling flexibility into their decisions and internal structures.

Corporate rigidity has enabled large, complex organizations to be stable. Rigidity in organizational structure and decision-making processes also meant slower adaptability to shifting and fluctuating external factors. This was one of the explicit factors creating the start-up culture of recent decades. Smaller, highly nimble start-ups were quicker to market with innovative products and services. But, for the most part, larger organizations could offset their slow adaptability weaknesses with financial and market strength. Exceptions like BlackBerry, Motorola, Blockbuster, Kodak, and others made great headlines and even better business case studies. But these mammoth failures were few and far between.

The impact of the changes wrought by the global pandemic means financial and market strength are no longer enough to offset the woes and penalties of rigid internal structures and outdated decision-making processes. Even large organizations will be susceptible to slow deaths from a thousand cuts. Only now those institutional deaths, whether by collapse or being consumed by another massive organization, will be speeded up via employee attrition, obsolete decision-making practices, and obstinately sticking to traditional internal structures and hierarchies.

In a perfect world, everyone would have the right team in place, the right experts on standby, and the right plans ready to execute. Such an ideal situation seldom transpires. And for the foreseeable future, it is less likely than ever before. Thus, leaders must be willing and able to adapt to evolving changes while keeping a steady eye on goals and desired outcomes.

Future success will require quick decision making in evolving situations epitomized by incomplete, insufficient, and often conflicting information. The essential criteria for success in this environment: a commitment to obsessive and excessive planning, replanning, and more planning. Enhanced with built-in adaptability.

Pre-Emptive Adaptability

Being adaptable is the ability to adjust to changing or evolving circumstances with agility and robustness. This is a highly marketable personal skill and an essential organizational competence in today's world. Simply put, being adaptable is mandatory for both leaders and the teams, departments, or organizations they lead.

In the past, being adaptable was a reflexive and responsive skill. Today, it must become a planned, deliberate, and premeditated proficiency.

The key way adaptability has changed as a leadership skill is in planning and preparing for it. No longer is it sufficient to put a SWOT team together to hurriedly devise a plan of action when a change in execution is needed. Panicking and reacting in moments of crisis seldom produce the best solutions. What is required today is a type of dynamic planning, fortitude, and a leadership evaluation methodology previously unnecessary.

The essence of dynamic planning is formulating strategic and executional plans subject to change and changing conditions. No more setting plans in stone. This is scenario planning taken almost to the extreme. Forget about Plan A coupled with Plan B as a backup. Think now in terms of Plans A, B, C, D, and maybe even E. And also, in terms of Plans A, B1, B2, C1, C2, and C3, the numbers indicating derivatives and alternatives for the substitute plans denoted by the letters.

Managers and leaders have long been evaluated on their abilities to deliver against a plan. Going forward, managers and leaders should be evaluated on their planning processes, including the ability to design plans B, C, D, and E. Yes, it means making plans that will never be delivered. But, more important, it means having plans in place when adaptability is required due to changing circumstances and conditions. As Dwight D. Eisenhower said, *"Plans are worthless, but planning is everything."*

Rather than annual plans tied to a fiscal year, it is better to have a rolling plan that is updated every quarter. These must include contingency plans to be triggered quickly by specified events and executed rapidly without time-consuming, chain-of-command delays.

With such contingency plans in place, the speed of decision making and resource allocation in response to a triggering event enables responses to happen quicker, with greater agility, and, most important, using pre-planned forethought. That is much better than reacting to changing events and conditions in real time and without adequate preparation.

Of course, having such agility and adaptability in place will be extremely challenging to leaders used to an annual strategic planning cycle. Now strategic planning is an ongoing occurrence rather than a once-a-year event. To paraphrase the 18th Century nursery rhyme: Leader be nimble, Leader be quick.

Knowing in advance when and how to tweak execution when potential or anticipated internal or external changes arise is crucial. Plans need to be designed, built, and executed on plausible futures, not certain ones. Imagine how differently organizations would have fared if they had an employee retention plan created around the plausible scenario that many workers would prefer a work-from-home option. Or if they had anticipated the very reasonable expectation that most office workers would favor some kind of hybrid working opportunity.

Unfortunately, few organizational leaders anticipated these highly conceivable circumstances arising and hence have been scurrying around trying to cope with and minimize the impact of the Great Resignation on their businesses.

When leaders stick to their predictions, they limit themselves. Sticking rigidly to set goals, deadlines, and execution plans despite changing circumstances means being governed by these arbitrary constraints. Your hands become tied and your options are limited. Adapting and improvising, within a system of identifying reasonably foreseeable events, expands your universe of possibilities. It is better to be goal guided than goal governed.

The key is to have great clarity of direction combined with an even greater execution flexibility. And, no matter how clear things may seem at the moment, do not get stuck in the presumed certainty of the present. That is a trap to be ever watchful for.

Plausible – Not Predictable – Futures
Leaders need to plan for plausible – not predictable – futures.

The airline industry is an example of how not to be adaptable and why the fast adaptation approach no longer works. It is an industry that thrives on predictability and suffers greatly during periods of turmoil and turbulence. It continues to be beset with a reactionary mindset easily waylaid by any disorder, tumult, and commotion in economic markets or socio-political conditions.

After laying off thousands of workers when travel came to a standstill in the early months of the pandemic in 2020, the industry was unprepared for the ensuing travel boom in late 2021 when the reins of lockdowns were lifted with declining covid cases. Despite billions in emergency government funding to help keep the industry afloat, airlines were woefully unprepared for the highly plausible scenario that people would rush to make up for the inability to travel for leisure or to visit families and friends over the previous 18 months.

Rather, the industry collectively *predicted* a slower take-off in latent travel desires and thus did not have the equipment, systems, or people in place to handle the *highly plausible* surge in passenger traffic. On New Year's Day 2022, nearly 5000 flights were canceled globally, mostly due to inadequate staffing and employee absences from the new strain of Covid-19. It was obvious that no plans B or C were in place, much less B1, B2, and B3 plans. Sadly, the industry remains inadequately prepared and insufficiently adaptable. Another 7000 flights were canceled globally over the Memorial Day weekend at the end of May 2022, mostly in the United States and the United Kingdom. Thousands more were cancelled or delayed across Europe and the United States in the first weeks of June 2022.

Making plans and decisions based on predictions is good. But limiting yourself to a single plan based on a single prediction is not. The optimal planning process is having multiple plans based on multiple plausible and conceivable potential scenarios.

Being adaptable, at an organizational level or even a workgroup level, comprises two elements: being prepared for an uncertain future and creating structured flexibility that enables employees to individually and collectively respond to uncertainty.

Being prepared:

- clear and well-communicated strategic direction
- the clear expression of the value each employee provides to the team and/or to a specific strategy
- transparent sharing of information (both the knowns and the unknowns)
- creating and constant updating of multiple execution plans with identified triggers for transitioning from one plan to another
- identifying the probable impact on employee health and wellbeing in each plan option

Creating structured flexibility:

- empowering small cross-functional teams to execute multiple implementation plans
- reducing or eliminating standard hierarchical structures and rigid organization charts
- building flexibility and options into internal processes
- ensuring continuous feedback on progress

- inculcating a culture of continuous learning for both personal and professional development

- creating internal processes and procedures for the sharing of information and lessons learned throughout execution of plans

- implementing internal financial reward and promotion systems that prioritize collaboration and group results over individual goals and objectives

In a highly adaptable culture, failure and result shortfalls are critical and acceptable components of ultimate success.

The biggest failure, however, is not preparing to be adaptable. Execution failures will be higher when flexibility and planned course corrections are not built into execution plans.

Building Your Adaptability Muscle and Mindset

Change at the organization or system level has to be accompanied by change at the personal level. It takes a three-step mindset approach to build your adaptability muscle:

Change is possible and I know I am capable of change.

Change is personal; therefore, I need to change.

Change is progress. I will grow or be rewarded by this change.

Adaptability requires the subset skills of initiative and risk-taking. While taking risks often makes leaders uncomfortable, even riskier is standing firm against a changing tide beyond your control or influence.

To date, most organizational structures have been designed for permanence and cost effectiveness. But their rigidity is not suited for flexibility and adaptability. This needs to change. There are many different ways of conceiving the structure of an organization at the individual, team, and organizational levels.

One model to consider for creating more flexible and adaptable teams is how hospital trauma surgery teams work. These teams comprise highly skilled and talented individuals working together for the common cause of saving a patient's life. Work is divided functionally between the doctors and nurses, with interchangeable skills (to some degree) within each group. Additionally, the teams work seamlessly despite having different members every day due to shift work, scheduling, and availability when the ambulance arrives at the emergency entrance.

Likewise, consider the "next man up" mentality of National Basketball Association teams. Fraught with injuries throughout the season, teams rely on players who are ready to step in at any moment when a teammate goes down. Even the star players may be called upon to play an uncomfortable position for several games while a teammate rests and recovers.

Another model to consider is the Hollywood Approach, a highly flexible and collaborative style explained in chapter 11.

There are three key components to building your personal adaptability muscle and mindset: increasing your ambiguity capacity, improving your internal self-chatter, and boosting your personal energy supply.

Your ambiguity capacity is the amount of ambiguity and uncertainty you can readily absorb at any given time. The more frequently you deal positively with ambiguity and uncertainty, the higher will be your ambiguity capacity.

Your brain is incessantly chatting to you. When this chatter is negative, you tend to interpret change, ambiguity, and uncertainty in a pessimistic light. Likewise, a positive internal voice will result in optimistic thoughts regarding change, ambiguity, and uncertainty. A negative internal voice impedes positive action. Likewise, positive internal self-chatter can ward off procrastination and stimulate positive action.

While positive self-chatter is good, it must be based on a realistic assessment of your situation. Overly minimizing the challenges in front of you, having unacceptable confidence levels, and being unrealistically optimistic can encourage detrimental action. This is what causes gamblers to believe their winning streaks will never end!

Every person, event, or situation we encounter is either an energy drainer or an energy booster. To maintain high levels of adaptability, you need to ensure that your physical, emotional, and mental energy levels are robust.

This entails ensuring sufficient mental and physical rest as well as adequate sleep. The greater your sustainable personal energy supply across all three energy spheres the better equipped you will be to adapt to the demands placed on you by a continuously changing world.

When it is obvious
that the goals cannot be reached,
don't adjust the goals, adjust the action steps.
Confucius

CHAPTER 8

Tenacity

Many of life's failures are people who did not realize
how close they were to success when they gave up.
Thomas Edison

U sually, when we think or talk about tenacity, it is in relation to overcoming hurdles and obstacles that get in the way of goal attainment. But there is more to tenacity, especially as a leadership skill.

Tenacity is the energy to keep driving forward. It is highest when you are passionate about whatever you are working on. Or whatever is driving you. When your passion fuels your purpose.

Tenacity is persistence with humility. It is not stubbornness, but rather the skill and willingness to keep trying, no matter how many walls you hit or obstacles appear in your path. Persistence means continuing to make an effort and seeing the value in making the effort, even after facing obstacles and setbacks.

Tenacity arises when you recognize that one failure does not make a permanent setback. It means you do not abandon an important endeavor just because unexpected hurdles or obstacles get in your way. Persistence means recognizing failures as additional opportunities to learn, grow, and progress. As Albert Einstein advised, "Failure is success in progress."

Tenacity does not mean continuing to do the same thing over and over again. It means continuing to pursue your objective, goal, or desire. By definition, it means being adaptable to changing circumstances to continue progressing toward your desired outcome.

When you are driven by passion, you are more likely to do the hard work and creative thinking required to keep hurdling over obstacles, pushing past self-doubts, and tossing aside the negative inputs received from others.

Let us now apply the concept of tenacity to people and how you lead people, including yourself. I promise you this notion of Humony Leadership will not likely line up with your preconceived notions of tenacity.

Tenacity Means Having People Patience

People are struggling more than ever. As mentioned previously, dealing with the uncertainty and ambiguity of today's times is difficult. Couple this with having to deal with lives turned upside down by the pandemic, either their own or their loved ones. We cannot expect co-workers and direct reports to silently close the door on the past two years and return to the workplace as if nothing has changed.

Additionally, the pandemic has taught us that people not only have lives outside the workplace – **they have responsibilities outside work**. Leaders and organizational policies must respect the reality of this truth. Humony Leaders understand that everyone's situation is different. They will be skilled in helping each person on their team achieve work/life harmony in ways that benefit the team members and the organization.

Leaders must anticipate that many, perhaps even the majority, of their team members will bring their fears, anxieties, uncertainties, and concerns with them as they return to workplace environments. They will be hesitant to commit to future changes and slow to adapt to new ideas and processes. This is normal and to be expected.

Leaders will need to amp up their people patience levels. This is a time to be encouraging, not demanding. You can help people on your teams and in your organizations by bringing positive energy, enthusiasm, and optimism into your conversations and communications. This is a time to slow down to speed up by focusing on the human aspects of your team members instead of the numbers on your spreadsheets.

People will need more time than previously to become comfortable. As mentioned before, everyone is effectively joining a new company, not returning to the previous one. Plus, thanks to the Great Resignation, many people are, in fact, joining new organizations. Remember that it takes time for everyone to become comfortable when joining a new entity, even when that entity has the same name and logo as before the pandemic. Whatever the name of your organization was before March 2020, you and your team members are now working for Your Name 2.0 and operating in the World 2022, not the world of 2019.

A key to successful people leadership will be exhibiting patience. Doing so shows others that you understand this is a different world and that people need time to adjust, adapt, readjust, and then readapt. And, know that what previously took one or two communications to implement change or achieve alignment may now take three or four. Going too fast will flame frustrations and resistance.

Finding New Ways of Working with People

Work relationships are all about communicating with others. Unfortunately, we get into patterns and habits in communicating with colleagues, peers, and direct reports.

What happens when you do the same thing repeatedly with someone, and yet this does not produce the results you want or need? Typically, you get frustrated. And obviously, something needs to change. But what?

Here is a clue: you cannot change the other person; you can only change yourself or what you are doing. Here is a story that illustrates the type of change that needs to be made:

> One of my coaching clients manages the monthly payroll for her organization. About five percent of the employees are in commission-generating roles. Another ten to fifteen percent are hourly employees. Thus, each month she needs her fellow managers to submit signed time sheets and confirmed commission details so that these employees are paid correctly and promptly.

> Most of the other managers get these details to her each month on time, while a few cut the deadline very close or miss it altogether. The latter cause her

and her staff to sacrifice personal and family time to ensure that the monthly payroll is accurately inputted in time for the direct deposits into everyone's bank accounts.

When I started coaching her, she expressed great frustration with those managers who were consistently late with their payroll data. She explained how she emailed "gentle reminders" in the days preceding the deadlines, yet each month two or three would submit their information several hours past the cut-off time. This had been ongoing since she had been promoted into her role a year earlier.

She and her team were too conscientious to allow late submissions to impact the monthly payroll payments of their colleagues. So, they worked overtime and became stressed and frustrated with their jobs and those seemingly uncaring department heads.

She wondered why those other managers could not or would not change their habits. What could she do, she asked in one of our early sessions? I told her she needed to change, not them.

She needed to change the way she reached out to these managers. Obviously, the email reminders were not generating the required response. She needed to change the way she communicated with them. In subsequent months she tried various other methodologies: calling, leaving voice messages, and sending IMs and text messages.

Not surprisingly, these new methods started working. Not across the board, but one by one. Some managers responded more quickly to text messages. Others were motivated into action by voice messages and phone calls, as they could hear the urgency and concern in her voice (which cannot be heard in an email). She realized that not everyone reads or quickly responds to emails, no matter how urgent and red-flagged they are.

She also started rewarding the prompt action of managers who submitted their payroll information on time. These were simple rewards, like bringing in freshly-baked muffins and bags of chocolates. She also started sending sincere thank you notes upon receiving the required information. She and her team even created the Payroll Friend of the Month Award and publicized this internally, which created a bit of friendly competition amongst the managers to be the first to submit their payroll data each month.

To change the actions and behaviors of others often requires leaders to change their own habits and actions first.

Accept What You Cannot Change

Of course, there are times that no matter what changes we make as leaders, others will simply not change. In such cases, we must accept this and figure out how to eliminate our personal frustrations through other actions. This is true in our personal lives, as well as in our professional lives.

Again, here is a story to illustrate:

I tend to be very organized and detailed when it comes to travel, both business trips and personal ones. I am known to make my hotel reservations 4-5 weeks in advance if I know a trip is confirmed.

However, one of my clients in Asia, is the exact opposite. He would schedule regional meetings or regional training sessions months in advance, but not make the final hotel arranges until a week or two before each event.

This was extremely frustrating for me, as I like to let my family and friends know where I will be staying. I also like to be able to arrange drinks and dinners with friends in the cities I am visiting, which is more difficult when I do not know where I will be staying. Especially in large cities like Tokyo, Bangkok, and Seoul where distances and traffic will determine how feasible it is to meet up with someone.

I tried for years to get him to change this habit and provide me with the relevant hotel details at least three weeks in advance. It just was not in his nature to do so.

So, rather than trying to change him, I worked on my own anxieties and frustrations that always built around this issue. I learned to accept the unknown details about hotel reservations. It meant making a lot more last-minute contacts and arrangements with friends, but as they say in basketball, "no harm, no foul." Everything always worked out in the end. And I learned a few new mechanisms for coping with frustration and mild anger.

Again, it is easier to change yourself than try to change others. Or change what you do instead of getting them to change their actions. Especially on minor things that are not worth the ongoing coaching and feedback discussions that motivate individual change. The bottom line is to know where to pick and win battles and when to devote your energy to more important matters.

Tenacity Means Not Giving Up on People

Most of the time, leaders so focused on results and solving problems start judging people solely on most recent short-term results and outputs. This is particularly true for first-time supervisors, team leaders, and managers.

I often have front-line leaders approach me on how to handle their direct reports who have 20-24 years in the organization and who appear to be unmotivated. These so-called clock watchers are often referred to as "retired on the job." The belief is they are simply working the bare minimum to stay employed until they can retire with additional benefits with 25 or 30 years of service.

These younger leaders are frustrated because their older, highly experienced, direct reports seem unwilling to take on additional responsibilities that would help their teams produce higher outputs and results. And, with their managerial labeling hats on, they claim these workers cannot be motivated to do more.

However, those employees were motivated at one point and previously performed at high levels. So, I challenge these young leaders to do more – to not give up so quickly on these experienced employees. I encourage them to find out:

Where is that old spark?

What happened to douse their motivational or performance flame?

How do you re-ignite it?

Talk to others who worked with them in the past.

What or who brought out their passion?

What aspect of their job did they once seem to enjoy most?

I also challenge these leaders to look within by asking them:

When was the last time you explained their Clear Line of Value to them?

When did you last discuss with them the potential, enhanced value they could bring to your team?

Working with dissatisfied or unengaged employees requires a series of conversations and interventions. People rarely change after a single conversation or intervention. It is an ongoing process requiring continuous feedback, acknowledgment of progress made, encouragement, and reassurance.

If they are truly in over their heads in their current job responsibilities, find another place within a part of the organization in which they would be a better fit and able to make a valuable contribution.

We should never give up on people. I realize that this is an idealistic approach. But, even when people appear to be a bad fit due to competency, confidence, or temperament, they are employable.

This is the bottom line: do not give up on those you lead. People are worthy of your time and effort. It sends a terrible signal to team members if you give up on one of them. Especially if you shunter them aside or "put them out to pasture," where others can see them withering away. Could this be their future fate?

Be Tenacious with Yourself

Discouragement seems to come easy for many. Our brains excel at grasping onto a single nugget of negative information or disappointment. Unfortunately, a regular diet of negative thoughts cascades into a downward spiral of confidence-busting moods and unconstructive perspectives.

A massive setback or an error in judgment does not lead to the end of your career. Mistakes are an iterative part of life. Mistakes will not define who you are. Responding and recovering from mistakes do.

Remember:

1) you only grow outside your comfort zone

2) your resiliency capability only grows from tenaciously pulling through challenging situations and rebounding from setbacks

Scientists have yet to invent a tenacity pill. Until they do, you must adjust your mindset to the positive zone and focus on potential solutions. Otherwise, problems will compound from negative thinking, procrastination, lowered self-esteem, and reduced confidence.

When setbacks occur, learn from them, pick yourself up (both mentally and physically), and keep going. Even when you cannot change things, accept what you cannot change (at this time). And when possible, change what you can.

You must be tenacious with yourself. Keep pushing yourself. Keep your goals and objectives in mind, especially those related to your North Star.

Focus on where you want to get, not the hurdles or obstacles blocking your path. Keep pushing when your gut instinct says to keep going. But also remember to take mental and physical breaks regularly to refuel your energy supply.

Lastly, believe in yourself. Opportunities abound, even if elsewhere outside your current organization and workplace.

When Not To Be Tenacious

Not every workplace situation calls for or deserves tenacity. Tenacity is not:

> Staying in a bad situation, hoping it improves.
>
> Continuing to work for a jerk/bully when it is impacting your health or mental sanity.
>
> Giving up and doing what you are told in a disengaged manner. That is fortitude and survival.
>
> Continuing to push yourself beyond healthy limits. When you can look in the mirror and honestly say you have given the situation your best shot. That you have left it all on the field. Some experiences and lessons position you for a better future.

All of these might be acceptable practices short-term. None are examples of continuous, positive long-term tenacity.

You learn more from losing than winning.
You learn to keep going.
Morgan Wooten

CHAPTER 9

Building Strong Relationships

There is a difference between
being a leader and being a boss.
Both are based on authority.
A boss demands blind obedience;
a leader earns his authority
through understanding and trust.
Klaus Balkenhol

W hen you shift your mindset from being a boss (manager) to being a leader, your relationship focus changes from oversight to trust.

There is a huge difference between having subordinates and direct reports and having followers as team members. Managers have subordinates and direct reports. Leaders have interactive, participatory, engaged, and collaborative followers. Managers lead based on authority. Leaders lead based on involvement, motivation, and alignment with a stated purpose.

The best leaders build and manage relationships with intent and purpose.

Relationships must be built and maintained on trust. And reinforced through effective communications, both formal and informal. Communicating as a leader should not be done on an ad hoc, spur-of-the-moment basis. Unfortunately, however, it often is. The best communications are planned and reviewed.

Leading people requires agility, flexibility, and adaptability. The old approach of "this is my leadership style, adapt to it" has no merit with today's workforce. If you express a "my way or the highway" attitude, you will likely find many team members opting for the door. Millions of workers learned during the pandemic that there is more to life than working for an intolerable, dictatorial, power-hungry boss. No longer do employees need to adapt to their leader's style. Instead, leaders must adapt to the needs of their team members.

Communicating *with* employees means two-way dialogues. Communicating is not sending more emails, having more team meetings comprising one-way presentations, or posting more corporate information on your intranet.

The remote worker setting has made communicating feel more transactional. Work (especially in the U.S.) has always been more transactional than relationship-based. Remote working worsened this, especially with bosses lacking Humony Leadership skills.

Also, communicating as a leader is not solely about getting your message across clearly and succinctly. Delivering your message is only one aspect of communication. The two critical communication skills for leaders are questioning and listening. Understanding the importance of these two skills is a fundamental aspect of transitioning from a manager to a leader.

Leaders must build new and enhanced communication skills, especially in attention, listening, paraphrasing/repeating, and deep questioning. They need to learn how to listen with empathy and for what is not being said. And they have to ensure all others feel heard.

Leaders who do not listen will eventually be surrounded by people unwilling to speak and contribute. Smart leaders intentionally build and manage relationships by engaging others through excellent questioning and listening skills.

Additionally, the goal for leaders is no longer to be the smartest person in the room. The objective is for leaders to create the smartest room possible.

Employee Engagement / Relationship Management

Is your workplace full of the Working Dead? Those unmotivated, unhappy, disengaged employers who did not leave and join the Great Resignation? What are you going to do with them? How are you going to light a fire under them? And if they remain entrenched, will your managers and leaders become disgruntled and dismayed enough to walk out the door at the first sign of an opportunity for them in another organization?

For many years Gallup has been measuring workplace engagement. And their results have been very consistent: roughly 85% of employees worldwide are either "not engaged" or "actively disengaged" at work. Behind these shocking numbers are poor management, combined with a lack of trust in leadership and a lack of recognition by leaders for the efforts made by employees.

Too many jobs are designed as thankless or meaningless tasks. Meaningless excellence is an oxymoron. Meaningless jobs require no innovation or creativity and often very little thinking. As a result, organizations get what they deserve: disengaged and unengaged workers robotically and unthinkingly performing meaningless and thankless tasks that create nil or little value.

Just as we were all in the pandemic storm together (though not all in the same boat), we will all be in the post-pandemic whirlpool together. It is not so much that people's values have changed as their value prioritizations have been realigned and reprioritized. Leaders have to truly and deeply understand team members, including their reprioritization of values and their individual motivational DNA.

When meeting together in person, people conform to the existing workplace culture. Now that people have been away from the Mother Ship, their personal and individual characteristics have come to the fore and arisen to a greater extent. Leaders now have to deal with these personal characteristics and start to treat people as they want to be treated. And to understand whether the previous patterns of conformity will be renewed or revoked by today's more empowered and galvanized workforce.

Great managers are the key to employee engagement and reducing attrition. According to the Predictive Index People Management Study:

> 94% of people with great bosses have passion and energy for their jobs; and

77% of people with bad managers plan to leave their companies in the next 12 months.

Relationships are built on communications. How you communicate as a leader is one of the decisive elements in establishing, building, and maintaining trust. Hence, it is important to continuously review and evaluate how you communicate with the team, collectively and individually. It is important that leaders not leave people hanging waiting for updates. Be proactive. Overcommunicate. Otherwise, you become a major source of disharmony.

Trust

Leaders should start all human relationships based on trust. Do not make people "earn" your trust. Start with trust and advise people what it takes to lose your trust.

Trust is foundational to leadership. If a leader is not trusted by the people they lead – and their colleagues and peers – nothing else they do matters. You cannot be an optimal leader if you are not trusted.

Unfortunately, there is not a great deal of trust in the workplace place today. Surveys consistently show that well over half of employees do not trust their employer. For example, a study by Davis Associates revealed that 57% of employees have little or no trust in their leaders. A similar survey from EY showed that less than half of employees (46%) placed "a great deal of trust" in their employers, while 15% indicated they had very little or no trust at all in their employers. The remaining

39% said they have "some trust" in their employers, which is not exactly a ringing endorsement of their leadership.

Unfortunately, the lack of trust in the workplace is a two-way street. The lack of trust in employees by their managers reduces inclusion, productivity, innovation, and results. A 2021 study by the Workforce Institute found that a lack of trust by bosses directly impacts how employees have a sense of belonging (64%), their career choices (58%), and their mental health (55%). Additionally, 24% of the survey respondents said they had left a company because they did not feel trusted. I suspect this figure is higher for the millions who are part of the Great Resignation.

That same survey shared how employees believe managers can earn higher levels of trust: being dependable (52%), being honest (34%), actively listening (28%), providing helpful feedback (25%), and caring about employee wellbeing (22%).

The top five factors influencing the lack of trust in bosses globally were:

1. Is not open or transparent in communication
2. Is not appreciative / does not provide recognition or praise for a job well done
3. Does not communicate with me enough
4. Does not value my point of view
5. Does not make wise business decisions

As you can see, poor communication is at the heart of mistrust. Asking questions and actively listening to others are trust-building behaviors. People are more willing to trust you when you ask for their input and know you will listen to their ideas, suggestions, issues, and concerns.

Another definitive element of trust is vulnerability. This may seem like an oxymoron, but it absolutely is not.

The idea of vulnerability – a quality of openness and honesty about all of who we are, not only our successes – is getting a lot more airtime than it used to, with authors like Brené Brown extolling it as a hidden superpower. But, due to its long tenure of being used as a synonym for "weakness," vulnerability is not usually the first quality we think of to describe leadership, trust, or workplace excellence.

Fortunately, mindful leadership and experts from other fields are transforming how we think about and understand the importance of vulnerability as a trust builder. Leaders no longer need to fear not having all the answers. It is acceptable (preferred actually) for leaders to share their uncertainties, cares, and concerns with subordinates. However, this must be done from a mindset of strength (we will figure this out together) and not from a mindset of weakness (I do not have the answer and I am so afraid).

Vulnerability in the workplace was a rare trait pre-pandemic. The last two years have clearly taught us that as humans we all have vulnerabilities. We have also learned that individually and collectively we can overcome these vulnerabilities through resiliency, adaptability, and tenacity.

As a leader, being real, open, and honest with the people you lead, your colleagues, and your peers creates opportunities to build stronger connections and relationships. Humony Leaders use moments of vulnerability to help themselves and their teams grow and foster their resiliency and adaptability capacities with compassion and harmony.

The kind of trust that makes a team great is called vulnerability-based trust. It sounds something like this:

I messed up.

I do not know the answer.

I need help. Can you teach me how to do that?

I am sorry. What I said was out-of-line.

Vulnerability-based trust will change everything for your team and your organization.

Vulnerability is a two-way street in trust building. How you allow your team members to be open about their vulnerabilities will impact their trust in you as their leader. Pause and reflect for a moment. What are the behaviors of your team members that make you trust them?

Most likely, one of your responses will be reliability. Trust is built and maintained when you know they will deliver upon their commitments. Super. But that's your "managing for results" mindset taking charge.

Now let your "leading people" and "leading people development" mindsets take over. What do you want your team members to do? Most likely:

- Come to you when they hit a hurdle or obstacle blocking their success.

- Come to you when apprehensive about their abilities to complete a task or assignment.

- Come to you when they are deeply uncertain about an action to take or a decision to make.

- Come to you to discuss ideas and options.

- Come to you to share their worries about the ambiguous and uncertain situations they are facing.

In other words: come to you. Ask for help when needed. Seek coaching. Share their concerns and vulnerabilities. Because you can be trusted to help them (and not blame them) when they are in over their heads or when the uncertainties they face are too overwhelming for them to handle on their own.

If you know you can trust them to come to you in these situations, then you can trust them not to go off track and make incorrect decisions on their own. With such two-way trust, they will come to you sooner when difficulties are encountered or mistakes are made, rather than waiting until such problems or errors become major fires requiring immediate and urgent handling.

This also means you can continue to stretch and develop your people through delegated assignments and tasks without worrying that they will make mistakes that will blow back on you. Because you trust them and they trust they can come to you.

Respect

Respect and trust go hand-in-hand. Civility and respect for others is not a weakness. You do not have to be "tough" or "a hard-nosed driver" to produce outstanding results through others. In fact, you can get a great deal more accomplished by being a kind, compassionate, caring, and respectful leader.

Respect has one common characteristic with trust: you have to earn respect from those you lead. It does not come automatically with your title or your office with a window view. It used to. But again, those days are long gone.

As with trust, do not make people earn your respect. Leaders need to start with respect for the people they lead. Doing so will garner respect for yourself based on reciprocity, a much better foundation than the faux respect granted because you are in a position of perceived authority or power (the key word being perceived).

From a Humony Leadership perspective, the goal for leaders is to be a Respectful Leadership as defined by The Center for Respectful Leadership:

> *Respect is about treating others with genuine decency, civility, and courtesy, regardless of their rank, circumstances, or the situation being shared – simply because they are another human being.*

Respect has nothing to do with genuinely liking another person. You do not have to like someone to work with them, but a strong working relationship requires reciprocal respect. And you cannot lead people if you do not exhibit respect for them, not in today's world.

The lack of respect from power-hungry, authoritative, mean-spirited bosses has been cited in several studies as an underlying and even primary cause of the Great Resignation.

"Feelings of respect and disrespect are NOT the result of rational, cognitive, and thoughtful consideration. They are

simply 'feelings' triggered by the primitive, unconscious parts of our brains. If we are responsible for leading others, then we must acknowledge this truth and learn the skills of adapting to it. That's what Respectful Leadership is all about," notes Gregg Ward, Founder and Executive Director of The Center for Respectful Leadership.

When treated with incivility, people often halt work mode, disengage, and focus their mental energy on re-evaluating the relationship. These distracting thoughts are unproductive. They also lead to confirmation bias regarding the downward slope of the relationship and expectations of being treated with incivility.

Incivility is not just a workplace issue. It has become an enormous and escalating societal issue in many countries across the world. As Ward told me in a conversation, "*we are in a time with the most disrespect, disagreement, and uncivil behavior in the U.S. since the Vietnam War.*" He cites Keyboard Warriors, who feel comfortable lashing out at others via social media from the safety of their devices, as a major contributing factor to the growth of incivility in society. I would add the acrimonious, inflammatory, abusive, and highly partisan commentary gushing forth from the cable "news" channels and our elected "leaders" in Congress and state governments as additional incendiary factors.

Workplace leaders now have an obligatory role in reducing – and then eliminating – incivility and disrespect within their domains. There needs to be zero tolerance for such behavior. Ward talks about creating an Active Respectful Culture (ARC) as the antidote to trust-reducing workplace environments.

Humony Leaders will take the proverbial bull by the horns and immediately tackle this issue head-on by resetting expectations and standards for civility and respect within their spheres of influence and authority.

I have been counseling the people I mentor to establish the following standard:

> Henceforth, no negative comments about any other employee, contract worker, customer, vendor, supplier, or anyone else we deal with will be tolerated.

> This means no more talking about the "nerds" in IT or the "bean counters" in finance. No more negative comments about a person's lack of experience or the school they attended.

> No more negative adjectives that have hidden or spiteful connotations, such as "she's an aggressive person" or "he speaks well for someone from his background."

Yes, this is a high standard. Yet it is also an achievable standard, as long as the leader walks the talk, displays compassion when correcting unacceptable comments, and forgives the occasional slip-ups. None of us are perfect and everyone, including the leaders who institute this standard, will lapse when emotionally distraught or under stress. While not excusable, such imperfections are understandable and must be dealt with humanely and compassionately.

Unless, of course, you have a repeat offender who refuses to change because "that's who they are." In such situations, you may – and probably should – decide to "make them available to industry." However, you will want to do so with benevolence, kindness, and compassion – not only because this is the right thing to do but also because your other team members will acutely be watching how you handle this situation.

As I pointed out earlier in this book, people want to feel good at work. To do so, they need four things. The first of these is to be respected. Create a Humony Workplace Culture (see chapter 13) and you will find respect pouring forth between all team members. Do not be surprised when this leads to higher productivity, innovation, collaboration and, of course, target surpassing results and achievements.

Hard Conversations

Trust, respect, and even vulnerability are each formed through engaging in hard, yet crucial, conversations. Likewise, professional and personal relationships can be forged – or destroyed – through how you handle (or avoid) conversations around difficult topics, including feedback, conflict, biases, wellbeing, and the social issues impacting your employees or their work performance.

You cannot establish or preserve trust by avoiding or procrastinating over having hard, difficult conversations. Yes, these are awkward and uncomfortable. But so is stewing over unresolved issues, allowing conflict to simmer, or coping with inadequate performance.

Leaders need to skill up for being uncomfortable. Being uncomfortable is a positive trait of vulnerability. The key is to turn discomfort into your new powerful leadership skill. The first step is knowing the intention of the conversations you hold. Intention creates confidence. Confidence creates better structured, effective conversations.

The critical question is not whether you should or should not have conversations on uncomfortable topics, especially the societal-related ones. The important question is whether you have the right, conducive environment for engaging in such discussions. Here are three essential questions to contemplate:

1) What will be the purpose of the conversation?

2) Does the foundation of trust, vulnerability, and openness within your team provide the requisite support for having the conversation?

3) Would having the conversation build or enhance a foundation of trust, vulnerability, openness, and understanding within the team (or between you and the other person if this will be a one-on-one conversation)?

There are many reasons or purposes for such conversations, including airing opinions and concerns, counseling the team, discussing the impact on individuals or team chemistry, or the impact on emotional or mental wellbeing. Getting this right, especially for conversations on the issues impacting society (and thus your staff), helps set the tone for the discussion. It also helps you prepare to lead the discussion, including how you will bring the conversation back on track when side issues arise.

Preparation to lead these discussions is essential. Unless unavoidable, they should not be held on a spur-of-the-moment basis. You need time to collect facts and understand the varied perspectives surrounding an issue. You might also need to grapple with how you feel about the issue.

You should plan how and at what point in the conversation you want to share your viewpoint. What questions do you want to ask to keep the dialogue flowing? How will you facilitate between differing viewpoints without showing favoritism or partiality? How will you ensure everyone has an opportunity to be heard, especially the introverts on your team? How will you safeguard against one or two domineering people overshadowing the voices of others?

Of course, these conversations are easier when the group has similar feelings resulting from a shared experience (the 9/11 attacks, a natural disaster, anxiety over uncertainties resulting from a global pandemic, etc.). These are much harder conversations when there are differences in the emotions, perspectives, feelings, or life experiences related to a highly volatile social situation.

The purpose of these conversations is not to seek agreement but rather to allow the airing of differences to attain a better understanding of how colleagues feel and think about events impacting society or their lives. Understanding the perspectives and viewpoints of others is a sign of respect. Sharing these in a collective setting in a harmonious work climate, or a one-on-one discussion with one's leader, builds awareness, comprehension, and trust. That is much better than allowing misunderstanding, the reinforcing of biases, or distrust to continue.

Providing Effective Feedback

Why do managers and leaders shy away from difficult feedback conversations?

One reason is that no one teaches them how to have these conversations and make them effective. Yet this is the ONE conversation you must absolutely never shy away from as a leader.

Many leaders, particularly first-time supervisors, team leaders, and managers, are uncomfortable having feedback conversations. When asked why, their replies are typically two-fold: a) we pay people good money to do good work, so why do I need to give them praise and b) I am afraid of how they might react if I have to give them constructive feedback or tell them they are not performing up to expectations.

Providing effective feedback requires a mindset change. First of all, you want to share feedback, not give feedback. Sharing denotes having a feedback conversation, not a one-way feedback directive and monologue.

Additionally, the purpose or intention of sharing performance feedback is to build confidence and capability in team members by:

- Reinforcing actions or behaviors that a person is doing well so that they will do so more often or in other circumstances.

- Helping them find ways to change behaviors that are having a negative impact in the workplace.

186

- Helping them identify and implement ways to improve performance, enhance current skills, and increase self-confidence.

There is nothing negative about these three intentions. The best mindset change you can make is eliminating the terms "positive" and "negative" from your vocabulary describing feedback. If your intention is to help your team member improve their behavior, performance, or confidence, then there is nothing negative about the feedback you will share.

Change your thinking. Feedback is either fortifying or enhancing – not positive or negative. Fortifying feedback reinforces behaviors and actions while building confidence and competency. Enhancement feedback aims to improve behaviors and actions while also building confidence and competency.

One of the benefits of this mindset change is that there is no longer a need for leaders to be hesitant or to procrastinate when there is a need for Enhancement Feedback, as there currently is for "negative" or "constructive" feedback. Since your objective is to help the team member improve, the inclination for hesitancy or procrastination is eradicated.

Do not open and close feedback conversations with toss-aside compliments (the sandwich or bookend approach). Be direct, truthful, and straight. Be sure to focus on the impact, not the behavior or the performance.

The sandwich approach to feedback makes the recipient feel manipulated. Research published in *Management Review Quarterly* in 2018 shows that the bookend approach to feedback almost always fails to correct negative or subpar performance.

One reason for this is that the recipient focuses more on how the feedback was delivered than on actual performance feedback specifics.

A study from 2014 showed that including one sentence when delivering constructive feedback can increase effectiveness by up to forty percent. That sentence: "I am giving you these comments because I have very high expectations and I know that you can reach them."

Remember, team members want reinforcing feedback. They want to know how and when they are producing good work. Hence, the motivational aspect of Fortifying Feedback is high.

There are eight core components for sharing effective feedback:

- It needs to be an ongoing process, not something done on an ad hoc basis. And it should be done in a timely manner related to recent output, how a task was handled, or when witnessed behavior needs correcting or modifying. Timeliness regarding a specific incident or before the next likely occurrence is critical.

- It needs to be provided frequently, not sporadically or only annually during the formal performance review process.

- It must be delivered and shared with the right intention (see above).

- It has to be relevant to the person's tasks and responsibilities.

- It has to be specific, not vague.

- It must be actionable.

188

- It has to be an interactive process.
- Progress must be monitored and reviewed regularly.

The best methodology for providing effective feedback is to keep Fortifying Feedback and Enhancement Feedback as separate conversations.

Trying to sugarcoat Enhancement Feedback with pat phrases such as "You are a valued employee, but" only weakens your delivery and no longer works. Everyone knows that "but" or "however" are going to follow opening phrases like "you are doing a good job" or "you did a good job on that task." Everyone knows the hammer is coming down after these perfunctory sentences, so they do neither the employee nor yourself any good. And it makes the leader appear less than authentic or trustworthy.

Rather, have one conversation when you need to share how well someone is doing. Then have another conversation when you want to share with them an area needing improvement.

Explaining the importance and impact of the person's actions and behaviors is the most frequently overlooked or omitted step in sharing feedback, which is why most feedback is ineffective. Without understanding the impact their behaviors or actions are having, there is little internal motivation for the person to make a change. This is why it is extremely important to explain both the impact and importance and to ensure the team member understands these. Part of the explanation of importance and impact is to clearly explain the implications and consequences of not making a change.

Feedback should come from a place of accountability, empathy, and learning. Accountability in a respectful, helpful, and actionable way. A healthy striving for continuous improvement goes to the core intention of effective feedback. Helping people grow while achieving individual and team goals creates team members better positioned and equipped for future success.

The other mindset change for leaders is to understand that everyone has the right to decide whether to change their behavior or actions. We cannot change others. We can merely point them in the right direction and encourage them to do so. However, we also need to point out clearly that they will be held accountable for their decisions to change or not to change. There are, of course, some exclusions where the choice to change is non-negotiable:

- Ethical matters
- Legal matters
- Safety issues
- Compliance policies
- Socially inappropriate behavior or comments
- Processes that must be followed
- Anything with major financial risk implications

Importance of Recognition

It is also important for leaders to acknowledge progress, small successes, and incremental wins. Change happens best when leaders recognize effort and reward results.

Unfortunately, many leaders do not do this for fear people will become complacent and slow down. Instead, they push, push, push. Not surprisingly, burnout increases significantly. Results are not achieved. Employee attrition increases. Those remaining become more stressed. And workplace harmony is nowhere in sight.

Humony leaders practice gratitude. They know that by openly celebrating successes and wins, team members will instinctively increase their efforts. Recognition of effort is highly motivational. Recognizing progress replenishes people, refuels their energy levels, and reignites their passions. That is much better than having a team of burnt-out souls struggling to get through the work day.

The rule of recognition is simple: Your default setting is to focus on what a person does right, and make a point to commend the person for those positive actions, sincerely and specifically. The three key benefits of this are:

- Encourages the person to continue those positive behaviors
- Builds trust and psychological safety
- Makes it easier to share Enhancement Feedback in the future

Building Your Relationships Authentically

Relationships should be built and strengthened based on authenticity. Too often, leaders with a manager's mindset attempt to be friends with everyone they lead, thinking that their direct reports will be more likely to do what is asked because the boss is friendly and nice.

Likewise, some leaders will feign interest in the personal lives of their team members, thinking that doing so makes them a "people person." Employees can smell these fake maneuvers a mile away.

You are who you are. That does not mean you cannot change. But the change has to be authentic. And gradual. You cannot move from one end of the spectrum to the other overnight. It is a long continuum from being a manager overzealous with power and control to a leader highly skilled in emotional intelligence and strong interpersonal communication skills.

There is a difference between being tough-minded when it comes to decision making and being tough-minded when dealing with team members. Replace the desire to show "tough love" to an employee with a willingness to express compassion and enhancement feedback to a human being who happens to be on your team.

This does not mean that straight-talk conversations should not be held, particularly with someone whose performance is not up to expectations. The difference is in the manner in which the conversation is held. This includes the tonality you use as well as how balanced you are in expressing your viewpoints and in soliciting inputs and possible corrective actions from the team member.

You can be compassionate and still hold people accountable. You can display empathy and still point out ways a person can improve their performance or their behavior. You can be gentle and kindhearted while helping someone understand the impact their performance or behavior is having. As long as you do so authentically.

However, building or maintaining collaborative relationships is hard if your attitude, behavior, or words interject friction into interpersonal interactions or experiences.

Another important step is to build your relationships beyond your direct reports. Having relationships at multiple levels throughout the organization is an essential best practice for being a better leader today and augmenting your career opportunities. As Reid Hoffman, the founder of LinkedIn, was famous for saying, *"in an era where things are continually changing, who you know is becoming more important than what you know."* This was an essential foundation for the growth of LinkedIn.

One good routine is having frequent skip-level discussions with those reporting to your direct reports. And always be asking, "what should I know that people are not telling me?"

Additionally, be sure to connect on the personal side of team members, peers, and those above you in the organizational echelon. This is best done by shifting your focus from getting to giving, providing help, feedback, and insights that help others perform better and make more optimal decisions. Helping people move through and transcend their challenges and problems makes you a more valuable colleague and leader.

As I have written throughout this book, this is not a short-term strategy to get you past the first few post-pandemic months or years. This is a permanent change in the way you need to lead people. There is nothing short-term about the changes stemming from the pandemic.

How people think about the relevance or importance of work (and even careers), how they view their options for earning money, and how they weigh the materialistic and non-materialistic aspects of their lives have fundamentally changed. If the thinking of your employees has changed, you would be foolish as a leader not to change your thinking on how you can be an effective and authentic leader.

And most importantly:

Rediscover your humanness.

Awaken the humanness inside you.

We can improve our relationships with others
by leaps and bounds
if we become encouragers instead of critics.
Joyce Meyer

CHAPTER 10

Wellbeing
and
Stress Management

No time for health today,
no health for your time tomorrow.
Irish Proverb

The mantra of more, more, more is not healthy. Nor is it conducive to workplace wellness.

Poor employee health is estimated to cost U.S. employers $530 billion per year and 1.4 billion work days of absence and impaired performance, according to a 2018 report from the Integrated Benefits Institute, a nonprofit health and productivity research organization.

The ability to proactively lead workplace wellness and the wellbeing of one's self and others is an important new skill. It is such an important topic that every month I share with my clients links to dozens of articles on mental wellbeing, stress management, brain health, and mindfulness. You will find these links in the Resources Section of the Caliente Leadership website.

Wellbeing is not only about protecting lives but also about improving the overall wellness of employees, contract workers, and temporary staff. Workplace wellness results from education, information, and encouragement. A Culture of Wellness should include emotional, mental, spiritual, environmental, and physical aspects of wellbeing.

A Culture of Wellness is one in which employees are comfortable and secure in asking for help! Sadly, this is not the case today. In a 2021 study conducted by workforce analytics firm Visier, 42% of women and 30% of men confirmed they feel uncomfortable talking to their immediate boss about burnout.

Not only is increasing workplace wellness the right thing to do, it also has an enormous impact on bottom-line profitability. According to the World Health Organization (2021), the global economy loses about US$1 trillion per year in productivity due to depression and anxiety. Even before the pandemic, the American Institute of Stress estimated that work stress alone costs U.S. businesses $500 billion annually. These are not insignificant sums of money.

Surprisingly, the importance of workplace wellness is not a new phenomenon. A decade ago, in 2012, an article in the *Harvard Business Review* reported that workplace wellbeing leads to 46% higher job satisfaction and 32% more committed and engaged staff. Two years earlier, the World Economic Forum reported that leadership wellbeing enhances managerial and leadership performance. That same report also cited a 50% increase in creativity and innovation and a 40% increase in employee engagement in organizations that emphasize leadership wellbeing.

Sadly, those early studies into workplace wellness and employee wellbeing provided an insufficient impetus for organizations to place these topics near the top of their priority lists. This must change. Not only for the health of employees but for the health of organizations, especially those hemorrhaging from the effects of the Great Resignation.

The American Institute of Stress (AIS) reported in 2019 that "job stress is far and away the major source of stress for American adults and has escalated precariously over the past few decades." In addition, AIS estimates that 120,000 people die every year as a direct result of work-related stress.

Other AIS statistics are both shocking and revealing:

- 40% of workers reported their jobs as very or extremely stressful

- 25% view their jobs as the number one stressor in their lives

- 20% of workers felt quite a bit or extremely stressed at work

- Job stress is more strongly associated with health complaints than financial or family problems

- Nearly half of workers say they need help to learn how to manage stress, and 42% say their coworkers need such help

- 19% had quit a previous job because of stress pre-pandemic

This is not solely a United States phenomenon. Government data shows that work-related stress and mental illness accounted for over half of work absences in the U.K. in 2019 and cost British businesses an estimated £26 billion per annum. While this pales to the estimated $500 billion per annum that workplace stress costs employers in the U.S., there is little doubt that workplace stress significantly impacts profitability and productivity throughout the world. We are all suffering the symptoms of the pandemic of stress sweeping the world today.

In Australia, workplace stress is a negative A$14.8 billion hit on that country's economy. Plus, stress-related presenteeism and absenteeism directly cost Australian employers over A$10 billion a year. Additionally, 3.2 days per worker are lost each year through workplace stress.

The same effect is seen in Europe, where nearly one in five European workers reported that they endured stress at work every day before the pandemic. Sadly, almost 14% of the employees who took part in The Workforce View in Europe 2018 study believed that their company "has no interest in their mental wellbeing at all."

Additionally, 51% of EU workers say stress is common in their workplace, with the cost of depression due to work estimated by the United Nations at 671 billion euros annually. With 25% of EU workers saying they felt emotionally drained by work during the enforced work-from-home situations, trade unions launched a campaign in 2020 for an EU law to tackle work-related stress amid "a mental health crisis" worsened by the pandemic lockdowns.

Putting in long hours at work is often associated with a strong work ethic and higher productivity, though it is unlikely to be indicative of either. Wellbeing needs to be embedded in the workflow. Unsustainable overwork should no longer be part of your operating model.

From a workplace perspective, stress, pressure, deadlines, tiredness, and relationships with coworkers can lead to increased emotional hijacking instances. Add to this the anxiety and concerns about returning to the workplace environment when the pandemic is under control means workplace environments will be more stressful than ever. As you will read later, increased stress directly impacts professional and personal decision making.

It is thus not surprising why so many workers are opting out of returning to workplaces they view as toxic, demeaning, and hazardous to their mental, emotional, and physical wellbeing. Thanks to the pandemic, people realize that wellbeing is not the absence of illnesses, diseases, aches, and pains but rather a holistic aggregation of being well physically, mentally, and emotionally.

We must leave behind the pre-pandemic ways of working and living. It is time to build habits and relationships that truly help us thrive. And a big part of that should be recalibrating our relationship with technology, including discontinuing activities and habits we picked up during the pandemic that leave us feeling drained and dcplctcd.

Workplace Wellness

Numerous research studies have shown direct linkages between workplace wellness and both employee engagement and employee retention. Sick workers do not show up to work and thus productivity and results are impacted. This makes intuitive sense. After all, without wellness, employees cannot do their work. Healthy workers translate into healthy organizations, which in turn create healthy economies.

Workplace wellness enables teams and organizations to transition to higher performance. Prior to the pandemic, the focus of employee health was almost solely on workplace safety. This notion of employee wellbeing started to be extended into the realm of psychological safety as the pandemic unfolded. Today, it must encompass much more, including the issues of burnout and mental wellbeing.

Today's workforce is no longer interested in small perks – ping-pong tables and free beverages – to compensate for workplace environments impacting their wellbeing.

Workplace wellness is not a checkbox activity. Nor is it a suite of employee assistance programs that provide access to professional help and other services. Workplace wellness needs to be an all-encompassing culture that inculcates the physical, emotional, and mental health of all employees as an integral part of the corporate culture.

Of course, organizations cannot mandate that employees take care of their physical, emotional, or mental wellbeing. All organizations and leaders can do is provide a workplace environment conducive to wellbeing. This includes minimizing the aspects of work and the workplace that are detrimental to wellbeing.

In doing so, workplace wellness must be inclusive but not mandatory. Everyone must have access to wellness education, support, and programs. However, participation must be voluntary. And, of course, you cannot allow criticism of those who choose to maintain an unhealthy lifestyle (for instance, being overweight or smoking). There can be no penalties or judgment for those who choose not to access or participate in wellness programs.

Additionally, while internal competition programs are good (i.e., step programs), these need to be flexible and adaptable to all employees. You also have to be careful that peer pressure is avoided so that no one feels forced to participate against their will.

Another best practice is to offer access to wellness programs outside the confines of the organization by extending these to gym memberships, martial arts programs, spin classes, nature walking clubs, nutritional coaching, and even holistic practices. The ideal practice is always to give employees maximum flexibility to decide what meets their individual needs.

The pre-pandemic concept of workplace wellbeing was built on a set of false assumptions, with a focus on treating the symptoms of unwellness instead of the root causes. Under the umbrella of Employee Assistance Programs (EAP), these often comprised:

Motivational workshops

Themed months around healthy habits

Fruit platters, protein drinks, and vegan snack options

Gym memberships

Exercise and yoga classes

On-site monthly shoulder and neck massages

Trendy breakout spaces with popular tech gadgets and games

Access to external mental health practitioners

Grief and family counselors

It was easy to be persuaded by consultants and magazine articles that these were the solutions to employee wellness. Unfortunately, too many companies fell into the "tick-box trap" of believing such programs were sufficient cure-alls.

It is obvious that such EAP initiatives are not enough. While a good start, they are inadequate to overcome or correct the root causes of workplace unwellness. Workplace wellbeing needs to start with:

Realistic workloads

Deadlines that do not require overtime or weekend work

Organization-wide education on coping, controlling, and managing stress

Removal of abusive and bullying bosses

Clarity of roles, responsibilities, and boundaries

Expressions of value and appreciation communicated clearly to each staff member

> Leadership and management trained to discuss burnout and wellness issues
>
> Concise and comprehensible communication on everything that impacts, or is likely to impact, the wellness of each employee
>
> Harmonious workplace environments

Funding gym memberships, providing healthy meals onsite, and "no meeting Thursdays" are bandages, not cures for workplace unwellness. To truly implement workplace wellbeing, leaders must stop overloading people, quit setting deadlines requiring overtime and weekend work, and remove abusive bosses from the workplace. It is that simple.

But again, workplace wellness goes well beyond the employee assistance programs mentioned above. You also have to take a hard look at the workplace climate you are responsible for as a leader, whether this is a team of six, a business unit of 600, or an organization of 6000. As Audrey McGibbon, founder of the Global Leadership Wellbeing Survey, notes, *"by lowering the risk of excessive work hours to levels beneath those associated* with *burnout and workaholism, you will deliver positive mental health and performance outcomes for employees, teams, and whole businesses."*

Again, it is the right moral and human thing to do. Additionally, if organizational leaders do not proactively fix toxic workplace cultures soon, governments will.

For example, the Workplace Relations Commission in Ireland has initiated a new Code of Conduct for businesses with the very apt title of the Right to Disconnect. The code has three essential provisions:

a) the right of employees not to routinely work outside normal business hours,

b) the right to not be penalized for not working outside those hours, and

c) the duty of employees to respect their co-workers' right to disconnect.

While failure by an employer to follow this Code is not yet an offense, the Code is now admissible in evidence in court proceedings, including the Labor Court and the Workplace Relations Commission in Ireland. Likewise, companies with 50 or more employees in France can no longer email employees after typical work hours. This labor law amendment legislates employees' right to disconnect and take full advantage of time off to distance themselves from the workplace during their off hours without fear of punishment.

These are examples of numerous government initiatives at the country and local levels mandating a shift toward a more humane workplace. As governments recognize the need for humans to disconnect and recharge, so too must business leaders.

The need to always be available to respond to work-related messages is taking a toll on employees' emotional and physical health. A study in Australia showed that employees who had supervisors expecting them to respond to work messages after work reported higher levels of psychological distress (70%) than those not required to respond to after-hours messages (45%). Additionally, those required to respond after work reported higher levels of emotional exhaustion (63% vs. 35%) and more physical health symptoms such as headaches and back pain (22% vs. 12%).

Leadership role modeling must be built into every workplace wellbeing culture. After all, what messages do workaholic managers send to their teams? What is the impact of late night and weekend emails or text messages on the mental health of team members?

A great example of preventing employee stress via late-night emails comes from one of my clients, Rodrigo S. Martineli, a global senior executive with more than 20 years in the technology space. At the end of each of his emails is this well-written and well-intentioned message:

> *TRULY HUMAN NOTICE: Getting this email out of regular working hours? We work at a digitally-enabled, relentless pace, which can disrupt our ability to sleep enough, eat right, exercise, and spend time with the people that matter most. I am sending you this email at a time that works for me. I only expect you to respond to it when convenient for you.*

Now that is an executive who puts people first. And it is a great example of reducing the pressure to respond to one's boss or colleague when an after-hours email pops into someone's inbox.

Four-Day Workweek *Don't get any ideas*

The five-day, 40-hour work week was established in the U.S. by the Fair Labor Standards Act in 1938. It is another artifact and relic from the pre-Information Revolution that seems antiquated and irrelevant to today's times.

France already has a 35-hour workweek, comprising five 7-hour days. As I write, there are trials of four-day workweeks in Australia, Japan, New Zealand, the United Arab Emirates, and the United Kingdom. In the latter, over 3300 employees in 70 companies are piloting a four-day work week with no loss in pay in what the program organizers call the world's biggest trial of a shorter workweek.

Will shorter work weeks reduce workplace drama and stress? We do not know yet, but hopefully these experiments will provide valuable insight. In Iceland, a pair of trials revealed that reducing weekly working hours led to better employee wellbeing, less stress, fewer sick days, and reduced burnout. Importantly, productivity stayed the same or improved. Now over 85% of Icelandic workers either work fewer weekly hours or have the right to do so. However, these two trials merely reduced working hours from 40 to 35 or 36 hours per week. They did not specifically test the notion of a four-day workweek.

One wonders how much of the standard 40-hour workweek is wasted time or spent clock watching. From running my own business for nearly 30 years, I can attest that productivity is rarely lost when working fewer hours. Less time often means greater concentration and fuller focus. Without the distractions of the typical workplace, I am convinced I get more done in less time (as the results in Iceland bear out). Hence, if only 10% of the time in the workplace is wasted (four hours per week), eliminating this gives you a four-day, 36-hour workweek. Food for thought.

But where else do you start in building a Culture of Workplace Wellness? Especially when there are so many aspects of workplace wellness. First, start by holding yourself accountable for supporting employee wellbeing. Second, I suggest two of the most impactful areas to begin with are reducing the impact of stress and burnout on your employees.

Stress

Stress is the number one factor impacting health in society. Workplace stress is the number one stress factor for a large segment of society, so this seems like a natural place to focus for improving workplace wellness and wellbeing.

Additionally, the American Psychological Association (APA) has identified Generation X (those born between 1965 and 1979) as the most stressed generation in history. This age group comprises the majority of the mid-level and senior-level leaders in organizations today. Hence, the most stressed generation in history is now leading businesses and organizations out of the most stressed period in recent history.

On top of all this, stress impacts decision making at all levels of organizations, causing less-than-optimal decisions to be made in reaction to people, situations, and events. This happens when the rational control center of our brains (the prefrontal cortex) is no longer in charge, having been overtaken by the emotional control center (the amygdala).

Stress and its impact on mental wellbeing did not start with the pandemic and certainly will not end with it. Covid was a wake-up call for understanding that employees are struggling and these struggles are resulting in mental unwellness issues. But without a doubt, people need help managing their daily stress, particularly work-induced stress.

Of course, not all stress is bad. Moderate and intermittent stress levels produce adrenalin, a chemical that improves short-term performance and increases alertness. As athletes are well aware, peak performance can be activated through moderate and short-term periods of stress.

Thus, feeling slightly nervous and anxious about an important presentation or meeting can prompt better performance. Hence, as long as the stress is not experienced for lengthy periods, it is generally harmless and can even be beneficial.

The same is not true for prolonged periods of stress or moments when stress levels are extremely elevated. In addition to increasing the risk of heart disease, depression, hypertension, and obesity, prolonged stress decreases cognitive performance. This impact can affect memory recall and cause disruptions to a person's decision-making processes.

When exposed to long periods of stress (as most of us are today), increased blood glucose and fatty acid levels significantly raise the risk of cardiovascular disease and diabetes. A study at University College London concluded that stress also raises cholesterol levels, another known factor that increases the risk of cardiovascular disease. In fact, stress can have significant adverse effects on our bodies, minds, emotions, and behavior as well.

While leaders need to accept and recognize that stress happens, they must know the differences between good stress and bad stress. And they must understand that mental fatigue impacts productivity and emotional stability, just like physical fatigue.

To counter the effects of workplace stress, leaders should implement organization-wide training and education on coping, controlling, and managing stress. You also have to remove the negative stigmas associated with mental unwellness and burnout.

But what if your organization does not take the lead on this? Then it is up to each leader to prioritize the mental wellbeing of the people they lead, including learning how to manage and reduce workplace and general stress. Here are a few places for you to begin:

- Study and use Purposeful Breathing techniques (see below) in your workplace and personal environments.

- Take regular five to 15-minute mental refresher breaks.

- Use your lunch periods for socializing and mental refresher breaks; not working.

- Encourage No Meetings Fridays (or Thursday afternoons) for you and your team.

Reducing Work-Related Stress

It is crucial to understand the normalcy of stress, particularly workplace stress. Everyone has moments of stress and most of us encounter some stress daily. Unfortunately, worrying about the feelings of stress or anxiety only serves to intensify and prolong those feelings.

Research shows that people who focus on their unique strengths and personal coping mechanisms (such as self-talk or recalling memories of past successes) in moments of stress can significantly decrease the strength and length of stress-induced feelings.

On the other hand, those who designate their stress-related feelings as a personal weakness and deficiency raise their levels of stress and anxiety and reduce their self-confidence.

Another method: stay connected with peers and friends. Networking and socializing are good for emotional wellbeing and quality of life. Many people isolate themselves, fearing that any inadequacies or self-doubts will be visible to others. This is particularly true for introverts.

Interacting with peers or friends is one way to allow yourself to be vulnerable and express tightly held fears in a safe and trusting environment. It is also a great way to be reminded that none of us is infallible or free of errors and mistakes, which can help reduce the angst surrounding the tougher decisions we face.

Focus on priorities. It is very easy to allow your calendar to be filled by others, get swamped by the minutiae of daily decision making, or be derailed by urgent matters taking priority over important tasks. Unfortunately, crossing out 10 or 15 small actions off your task list is unlikely to produce the significant outcomes achieved from one strategic decision or solution arising from an hour of focused contemplation and analysis.

I often wonder when the word priority became pluralized. In reality, we should have only one priority. Unfortunately, that has not been the way of the world for decades. Everyone has multiple priorities. However, as the pithy saying goes, "if everything is a priority, then nothing is a priority." My rule of thumb: more than three priorities equals a to-do list.

Years ago, I divided my to-do list into two separate lists, one of which has the 2-3 major priorities I am working on (such as writing this book) and the other containing my list of getting "stuff" done. That GSD list receives a greatly reduced prioritization in my life, other than when specific deadlines (like calling a friend on their birthday or the payment due dates on bills) give them immediacy or urgency.

If you do not focus on important priorities, they often become emergencies. Those who delegate more and micromanage less create more time for the priorities in their professional and personal lives. They also carve out more time and mental energy to contemplate the bigger issues and decisions confronting them.

Workplace stress and pressures cause tension to build up in our muscles. Here is a method for releasing and relaxing muscle tension. The key to this technique is to deliberately tense your muscles so that they will completely relax after this exercise.

1. Find a comfortable place to sit, preferably in a quiet location. Remove your shoes if possible.

2. Start with the muscles in your forehead and scalp. Take a deep breath and then tense all the muscles in this area for a count of four. Relax the muscles as you exhale.

3. Continue this tensing and releasing process, coupled with deep breathing, down to other areas in your body that feel tense or sore. Mentally travel throughout your whole body, from the top of your head to the tips of your toes. Pay particular attention to the classic stress accumulation points such as neck, shoulders, jaw, middle back, lower back, and feet.

Two other proven techniques for reducing the impact of workplace stress – mindfulness techniques and battling distractions – will be discussed later in this chapter.

Purposeful Breathing

The first step in controlling stress is practicing purposeful rhythmic breathing. As soon as your body sends stress signals (shortness of breath, sweaty palms, churning in the gut, overwhelming sensations in your mind), hit the pause button. Literally.

You can quickly calm your nervous system and regain control over your thoughts and emotions through purposeful breathing. Purposeful breathing can be done anywhere in the workplace — at your desk, in a meeting surrounded by others, while walking to or from a meeting, or during a quick visit outside to enjoy some fresh air and a bit of sunshine.

There are many techniques and methods for purposeful breathing. All of them focus on purposefully creating a rhythmic breathing pattern. None require you to take off your shoes, close your eyes (though doing so can help prevent distractions), or twist your body into a lotus position.

The important thing is to find and practice a pattern of breathing that works best for you. Practicing rhythmic breathing throughout the day also increases oxygen levels. When the level of oxygen reaching the brain increases, the brain responds by sending signals to the body to relax. Increased oxygen levels in the brain will also trigger the release of feel-good hormones (such as dopamine) that help relieve pain and increase feelings of wellness and happiness.

If you think mindful breathing has nothing to do with the workplace, consider the U.S. Navy SEALs. Facing some of the most stressful workplace conditions one can imagine, the SEALs use a four-part breathing sequence called Box Breathing. It is a technique that can be done in five minutes:

1. Find a comfortable chair or lie down.
2. Inhale for four seconds.
3. Hold the air in your lungs for four seconds.
4. Exhale for four seconds, emptying all the air in your lungs.
5. Hold your lungs empty for four seconds (no inhalation).
6. Repeat for five minutes or as long as necessary to feel refocused and relaxed.

Taking five to seven deep, purposeful breaths using the Box Breathing pattern during stressful moments provides me with an immediate sense of calm and perspective needed to handle a situation more contemplatively and with full focus. Since I use a shortened version of this technique, I count between eight and ten at each step.

Respond, Do Not React

The second step in controlling stress is learning to respond instead of reacting to people, situations, and events. There are major differences between reacting and responding.

Impulsively reacting tends to add more stress to both yourself and others. Reacting also usually results in the first thought or idea becoming a decision, which often is not the best possible solution.

On the other hand, responding is more reflective and helps redirect your thoughts to consider a range of options. Responding, particularly with the phrase "let me think about that," creates time for adequate reflection, analysis, and contemplation. It also decreases the stress caused from feeling pressured – by yourself and others – to make an immediate or quick decision. All of which will make you a better thinker and decision maker.

In my case, when someone asks me, "what do you think?" the phrase I use in reply is, "I think I need time to think about this." Having this as a prepared reply has benefitted my clients and me numerous times. For example, I was recently transiting through the Denver airport when a client I coach called me. He told me about a situation at work and wanted to bounce his planned response off me. Since the planned approach was good, I was nearly inclined to react with a "that sounds like an appropriate way to proceed" reply.

Fortunately, I hesitated and said instead, "I think I need time to think about this. I am about to board my flight to Houston. Is it okay if I get back to you in a couple of hours after we land?" He replied affirmatively, giving me time inflight to think through his situation and planned response.

When I landed in Houston, I called him and gave him some ideas that enhanced his planned actions. He thanked me profusely since these ideas, when added to his initial thoughts, were likely to produce a more optimal outcome for him and his team.

That is the power of learning to respond, instead of reacting, even in circumstances where there is no drama or conflict involved. It provides an opportunity for better and deeper thinking, which usually leads to better results.

Another technique to help you hold off the temptation to respond immediately in any given situation is to ask questions instead of making an on-the-spot decision. This is not a procrastination technique unless used incorrectly for the wrong reasons.

Great leaders excel at asking the right questions to help their team members determine the best solutions. Such leaders know it is better to develop others by asking the right thought-provoking questions than for the leader to have all the right answers in hand and make all the decisions.

This has five benefits for leaders:

a) less stress by reducing the need to have all the answers

b) increased empowerment of their team members

c) greater development of their team members

d) increased ownership and commitment to the solution determined since this has emanated wholly or partially from the team members

e) improved business results

First Responder Mode

I also want to encourage you to become a First Responder to situations, events, and people rather than a First Reactor.

Here is what I mean by that. Decades ago, I learned to scuba dive and became certified as a Rescue Diver. The first thing we are taught in the Rescue Diver certification program is to "respond, not react." There is no point in reacting and immediately jumping into the water when we hear a cry for help. Rather, we get trained first to assess a situation to see what dangers might be lurking (jellyfish, strong currents, floating fishing nets, etc.). Then, once we know we won't be putting ourselves or others in danger — and once we have ensured we have all of the appropriate gear with us — do we jump into the water and head toward the struggling person.

All this takes only a handful of seconds, but it prevents additional problems from cropping up. EMTs and others are trained to do the same, which is why they are called First Responders.

This is what we all need to do in today's world. Pause, assess the situation, and then respond rather than react. There is too much pressure for fast decisions, particularly in the workplace. Almost everyone is compelled to make snap decisions in First Reactor mode rather than better, more optimal decisions in First Responder mode. Another benefit of First Responder mode: it reduces the stress levels for all involved.

One way to do this is called cue-controlled relaxation. This technique uses a specific cue, such as a word or phrase, to evoke a specific and conditioned response. An example would be to use the word "pause" to remind and condition yourself to pause before reacting or responding. Or use the phrase "not while under stress" to remind yourself to become calmer and more rational before making a decision.

Burnout

Burnout is a state of complete emotional, physical, and mental exhaustion caused by excessive and prolonged work-related stress. Burnout costs organizations billions in terms of absenteeism, employee attrition, productivity, reduced employee engagement, and lower customer satisfaction. It is so prevalent that the World Health Organization (WHO) declared burnout an occupational phenomenon in 2019 (before the pandemic).

While the pandemic did not create burnout, it certainly aggravated and expedited its spread. In some ways, burnout is the new pandemic replacing the Covid one. In fact, the numbers related to the cost of burnout are staggering. The Wellness

Council of America surveyed employees and leaders at 228 companies in 2020, with the results showing:

- 90% of employers were concerned that their employees were experiencing burnout.
- 93% of employers believe employee wellbeing and support will be critical for attracting and retaining talent in the future.
- 45% of employees experienced symptoms of burnout in the past 12 months, but only 31% felt supported by their employer's mental health resources.

Additionally, 98% of U.S. and U.K. Human Resource professionals surveyed said they have felt burned out at work during the past six months, and 78% are "open to leaving their jobs." This does not bode well for stemming the Great Resignation outflow. When Human Resources staff start leaving, others in the organization are sure to follow.

In many ways, we are swapping the Covid pandemic for a burnout pandemic. This has huge short-term and long-term societal implications. Yet, an article in Forbes (November 2021) reported that 90% of managers are not worried about employee burnout. Talk about a disconnect!

If your work environment is so stressful and demanding that people use their time off to recover, you probably have a burnout culture. A healthy organization does not drain its people to the point that their days off are used for recuperation and re-energizing. These days need to be used for enjoyment, family time, and living!

Burnout results from both professional and personal factors, including:

Mental wellbeing struggles

Home life challenges

Increased level of unsustainable work demands

Care-giver and home-educator responsibilities

In the Visier research study in 2021 cited earlier, 89% of the 1000 full-time employees surveyed said they had experienced burnout within the previous 12 months. Obviously, the pandemic and the stress of on-and-off lockdowns and other social issues played key roles in this extraordinarily high number. But do not blame everything on the pandemic. The pandemic merely put burnout on an accelerated path. It was already becoming a major workplace issue before the pandemic, hence the reason for the WHO declaration in 2019.

Probably the most revealing statistic from the Visier study is that 70% of those surveyed said they would leave their current job for another organization offering better resources to reduce the feelings of burnout. Without a doubt, employees are struggling with burnout. They need the help of organizational leaders to learn how to prevent, cope with, and minimize the impact of burnout on their mental, physical, and emotional wellbeing.

Leaders and managers are also critical contributing factors to burnout. Leaders with responsibility for improving the wellbeing of employees are themselves fatigued and overwhelmed. Such overwhelmed and stressed-out leaders soon become the source of their team members' stress and burnout!

Burnout builds up over time, not overnight. It is similar to weight gain during the end-of-the-year festive seasons. No one wakes up in early January suddenly several pounds heavier than the day before. Rather, the weight builds up slowly from mid-November until New Year's Day, when the sudden realization hits that the number on the scale is higher than a few weeks ago.

Burnout is similar. It builds and builds slowly, day by day, week by week. Often it goes unnoticeable by the individual until they wake up one morning totally exhausted mentally, physically, and emotionally. This is why it is critical that leaders keep a vigorous lookout for early warning burnout signals. The person on the road to burnout is likely to overlook and miss these warning signs simply because they are too focused on their workload and deadlines.

Jennifer Moss, author of *The Burnout Epidemic: The Rise of Chronic Stress and How We Can Fix It*, says there are six workplace root causes of burnout: an unsustainable workload, perceived lack of control, insufficient rewards for effort, a lack of a supportive community, a lack of fairness, and mismatched values and skills. I would add to her list unclear communications from managers and a lack of managerial support.

The impact of burnout from work on employees is significant:

63% are more likely to take a sick day

23% are more likely to visit the emergency room

They are 2.6 times more likely to be actively seeking a different job

They are 13% less confident in their own job performance

It is time to aggressively tackle the terrible statistics about burnout and workplace stress. This is an unprecedented opportunity for leaders and organizations to make meaningful and long-lasting decisions to reduce the impact of workplace stress on long-term mental and emotional wellbeing. We must move past the poor assumptions and stigmas of the past in order to adequately advance individual and collective wellbeing on all fronts. This goes well beyond asking RUOK (the acronym for Are You Okay?).

Organizations must start to take primary responsibility for burnout prevention and management. A culture of overwork does not make people more productive – it makes them sick.

The causes of burnout are not a mystery. *"Burnout in the workplace is not a vast, complex tapestry that we still don't understand. It is a failure of employers and managers to address core problems plaguing their employees: workplace harassment, an overwhelming workload, a lack of appreciation, and a lack of hope for advancement and a better future,"* writes Ed Zitron, CEO of EZPR.

So, what can you do? Start by training all people leaders to recognize the early warning signs of burnout:

Growing alienation from work

Escalating and observable frustrations, particularly

in those who usually remain calm and collected

Increased cynicism

A decline in performance, particularly in those who are usually high performers

Compromised concentration

Reduced creativity and innovative thinking, especially in those who are normally your champions in these areas

Lack of positivity (particularly by those who are usually optimistic and confident)

Likewise, individuals must also learn to recognize these early signals of burnout and take appropriate action. Individual actions include establishing better boundaries, taking mental refresher breaks, increasing exercise, and frequently switching off from digital devices.

The other major step to take is to destigmatize burnout within your organization. It is vital to recognize burnout as a genuine mental wellness issue and encourage individual mental rest or mental refresher days for all staff. It is far better to have someone take a day or two away from work when they are on the precipice of burnout than to have them fall into the abyss of burnout and need two to three weeks of recovery time.

It is okay – in fact it is best – for leaders to show transparency and admit when they are exhausted, disengaged, or becoming cynical. Leaders need to exhibit and model the self-care behavior that works best for them. Leaders who do not take care of themselves are in no position to help their team members cope with the early stages of burnout.

All people leaders should be encouraged to openly discuss burnout with their team members. Gallup research shows that "employees whose manager is always willing to listen to their work-related problems are 62% less likely to be burned out."

Of course, many leaders are not properly equipped to have these conversations. As one leader told me, "I'm a manager, not a psychiatrist." That is the wrong mindset. You need not be a psychiatrist to recognize the early warning signs above. And you do not need to be a psychiatrist – just a people-centric leader – to have open and transparent conversations with staff about burnout and mental wellness issues.

Leaders are NOT mental health professionals. But they do not need to be. Leaders are conduits to the resources available to their team members, such as the organization's EAP options, telehealth, and local community support programs. They also need to recognize the early warning signs of burnout and proactively initiate nuanced conversations with team members. Unfortunately, most leaders and managers are ill-equipped to hold discussions on burnout, stress management, and mental wellbeing. Fortunately, the solution is simple: educate and equip them!!

One silver lining from the pandemic is that open workplace conversations about burnout and overall mental wellbeing are becoming normalized and accepted. As prolonged stress and fatigue impact more people, there is a newfound level of comfortableness and acceptance for admitting when one is not feeling well.

Mindfulness Techniques in the Workplace

Another critical way to reduce stress and burnout in the workplace is to incorporate some mindfulness techniques, both individually and collectively.

Mindfulness is an exercise in focus. The focus can be relaxation, emotional control, interpersonal interaction, cognitive problem solving, or decision making. Astute practitioners use mindfulness in each of these situations and many others.

The brain is wired to think. It is not possible to get the brain to stop thinking, much less to stop thinking about something stressful. The only choice we have is to exert control over the brain through the deliberate practice of focusing attention on one specific thing at a time (mindfulness) to prevent it from being activated by other, often stressful, factors. Mindfulness is a proven range of techniques for quieting that voice in your head for minutes at a time. Think of mindfulness practices as exercises for your brain.

The tricky part is deciding to become mindful. We are so used to operating in autopilot mode, rushing from one activity or task to another, that we have no internal mechanism to remind us occasionally to pause and become fully present.

Almost everyone has a tightly packed schedule these days. So, where is the time available to add some mindfulness practices throughout the workday? Fortunately, you do not necessarily need to free up great quantities of time during the day to practice being mindfully present. This section will provide a few ways to add mindfulness to what you are already doing; none of these require more than five to ten minutes to implement.

As always, it starts with breathing. Just breathing a little deeper for a few respiratory cycles at a time reduces the stress signals coursing through your body. Do this repeatedly several times a day and you will notice improvements in your attention span and stress levels. If necessary, use a smartphone app to send you random messages throughout the day to breathe deeply (purposeful breathing).

Awareness of your posture is another way to be mindful. Are you sitting up straight or slouching? Is your neck being strained? Are your leg muscles tight? Noticing the tension in your body can make you realize that you are unconsciously worried about something that you might not have known was troubling you. Improving your posture is great, but becoming aware of a hidden concern is even better.

A lot is being written these days about mindful eating practices. I do not think you need to go all Zen with your lunch each day. On the other hand, taking a few minutes to savor several bites without thinking about email or glancing through social media or news sites is a good mindful practice, especially if eating at your desk. Eating is another of those daily tasks we often handle on autopilot. And like most everything else done in a habitual, unthinking mode, eating provides an opportunity to pause, become centered and present, and switch into mindfulness.

Speaking of lunch, why not have a relaxing lunch break a couple of times a week? Eat outside if possible and comfortable.

Incorporate a short 20-minute stroll into your lunch period. Find a quiet place to sit with your thoughts (without judgment) for 10-15 minutes. Whatever you do, be sure to do it without any electronic devices — no checking emails, calendars, text messages, or social media. The point is to find a few minutes a couple of times a week for some peace and quiet, something very few of us experience enough.

In addition to breathing purposefully, you can enter mindfulness by walking with purpose. For most, the point of walking, particularly at work, is simply to get from one place to another. Change that by turning walks, even short ones, into opportunities to check in with yourself: any tension spots in the body? Is your breathing shallow or deep? Are you currently *mind full* or *mindful*? What is the single most important thought you should be having at this moment? What has happened in the past 24 hours for which you are grateful?

Focusing on core listening skills is another way to become more mindful at work. Great listening is a whole lot more than being silent while someone else speaks. Mindfully listening means giving your full attention not only to what is being said but also to the emotions behind what is being said. Listening in a mindfulness mode helps detect how strongly a person believes what she or he is saying.

Being fully present in the conversation also enables you to pick up on what is not being said and any hidden agendas in the room. Additionally, mindfully listening helps prevent you from interrupting colleagues or direct reports, resulting in higher satisfaction, happiness, and employee engagement among colleagues and team members.

Those who practice mindfulness while listening are also more likely to be receptive to original ideas and new information. This openness results in increased innovation and higher quality decision making. Also, it helps create a culture of collaboration and cooperation.

Some people use personal mantras or favorite sayings to push them into mindfulness moments throughout the day. These can be pithy sayings like "happiness begins with me" or motivational messages such as "I am competent, capable, and ready to handle today's challenges."

Others might be simple reminders of deep-seated beliefs. For instance, one of my smartphone apps sends me the message *I am moving forward* at random intervals throughout the day. It also sends me the message *Mind Full or Mindful?* several times a day as well. Seeing these messages reminds me to pause, take a few deep, purposeful breaths, and refocus my thoughts on the tasks and projects that are truly propelling me forward.

Practicing mindfulness at work can help you navigate interpersonal relationships and expectations to achieve optimal results or progress. It also helps you understand and accept that you may not always get desired or anticipated results. The key is to use mindfulness as a foundation for effective work and optimal performance.

The workplace is rife with difficult and tense conversations that bring forth an array of emotions. Mindfulness can help to decrease the temptation to unleash an emotional outburst through a technique called anchoring. Anything you can do to focus on your physical presence and your senses is a form of anchoring. One example is placing your feet firmly on the floor and observing how that feels. As is pushing your lower back firmly into the lumbar support area of a chair. Some people simply cross their fingers, clasp their hands, or clench their fists (beneath a table or desk, out of sight of others) as a physical reminder to regulate emotional reactions.

Another method for handling tough conversations is standing up and walking around the room a bit. Doing so activates the thinking part of the brain (prefrontal cortex).

For additional ways to incorporate mindfulness practices into your workday and workplace, see chapter 14 in *Better Decisions Better Thinking Better Outcomes: How to Go from Mind Full to Mindful Leadership.*

Battling Distractions
Your attention may be your most precious resource.

So why do we spend so much of the precious time allotted to us in an "always-on" relentless push to check off every item on our too lengthy to-do lists? Though we think of time as fixed, it is actually very relative. It is not just how much we have, but how we use it. We can live in a way that makes us feel time affluent, or we can live in a perpetual time famine. As Seneca noted, "*life, if lived well, is long enough.*"

Where you place your attention gets your energy (mental, emotional, and physical). Noise is the enemy. Distraction is the enemy. A lack of focus is your enemy. Clarity is the primary goal.

With clarity comes focus and attention. Be clear about what is important and critical to your organizational and personal success (focus on priorities over the urgent).

Otherwise, you suffer the opportunity cost from endless distractions, noise, and fire-fighting activity. The key: act with intention about your attention.

The workplace environment for most of us is one of constant distractions and interruptions (two major causes of workplace stress). Hence, our natural inclination is to resort to a mode of multitasking, which is NOT a viable long-term solution. Multitasking may be fine for simple tasks like deleting junk email while listening to a conference call. However, multitasking is the curse of focus and making good decisions.

To be purposeful and creative, you need to create mental space for yourself. Using a mindfulness mode increases focus, pushes away distractions, and enhances productivity and creativity. A mindfulness approach to increase focus entails:

1. Eliminating all potential distractions, including closing the email and Internet message programs on your computer and setting your mobile phone to airplane mode. Close your door if you have one (and have a Do Not Disturb sign on it if culturally acceptable in your organization).

2. Ensuring you have sufficient water, coffee, tea, or other drinks to last at least an hour.

3. Using purposeful breathing to prepare your mind to concentrate.

4. Clearing out all thoughts and ruminations, including the mind's chatter about the other tasks

you could be doing (write these down for reference later to help clear your working memory space).

5. Taking two to five minutes to focus on the task at hand completely, remembering to include the most desirable outcome, or picturing what success will look like, i.e., "I will finish the first draft of this report before lunch."

6. Getting to work. If the task will take several hours to complete, get up and take a short break every 50-75 minutes. Movement increases the circulation of blood, which is good for the brain. Use this time to replenish liquid supplies, grab a few minutes of fresh air, and think of something pleasurable.

   However, do not access email or engage in conversations that are likely to mentally distract you from returning fully focused on the task at hand. You do not want anything cluttering up your precious working memory space.

The brain repeats rewarding behaviors. When given a choice between two behaviors — one that is rewarding and one that is not — the brain will instinctively select the rewarding one.

If we pay attention to the dissatisfaction we feel when we are distracted, and compare this feeling to the positive feelings experienced when we are fully present, we can train our brains to see the relative rewards of each state.

The more we practice this, the more we can train our brains to fend off distractions for the more rewarding experience and feeling of being mindfully present.

As the demands for your attention become increasingly seductive, it is vital to be highly conscious of how you invest your attention. By taking a moment to slow down and consider your true priorities, you will be better positioned to determine how to capitalize on your limited attention resources by focusing on what is important to you.

Mental Health

Mental wellness is a fundamental aspect of a healthy lifestyle. And mental wellness is impacted by the workplace environment – whether that workplace is a co-located space or a working from home situation.

Even before Covid-19, mental health was recognized as a social issue with business implications. Worker anxiety and depression are tied to increased absenteeism rates, employee turnover, distraction, and poor performance on the job. According to the World Bank, the global economy loses about US$1 trillion annually in productivity because of depression and anxiety.

Additionally, mental, neurological, and substance-use disorders are estimated to cause worldwide economic output losses of $2.5 trillion to $8.5 trillion annually.

This occurs even though every $1 invested in scaled-up treatment for common mental disorders, such as depression and anxiety, yields a $5 return in improved health and productivity, according to the World Health Organization, United for Global Mental Health, and the World Federation for Mental Health.

No wonder mindfulness training in the workplace is now being adopted by a wide range of companies, including Aetna,

Apple, CBRE, Changje, Deutsche Bank, General Mills, Goldman Sachs, Google, HBO, Intel, LinkedIn, Nike, Prentice Hall Publishing, Proctor & Gamble, and Sony. The reason for doing so is often two-fold: to increase productivity and to provide employees with valuable life skills. As Lindsay VanDriel, a platform strategist in Intel's Software and Services Group, stated in an internal newsletter, "*The idea is to give people a set of fundamental skills that they can use at any time, anywhere, to help them deal with stressful situations.*"

You cannot burden people with constant change, rapid transformations, and the never-ending push for increased results and expect them to be okay mentally and physically. The lack of time to exercise and the bad eating habits related to stress relief means work has been a major contributing factor to today's obesity rates. The same goes for today's increasing mental health issues.

Research from Tufts Medical Center and One Mind at Work estimates that depression accounts for an estimated $44 billion in losses to workplace productivity.

The notion that companies should be responsible for employees' mental health is relatively new. Most CEOs and senior leaders today — the vast majority are either Boomers or Gen X — grew up in corporate cultures rife with stigmas around depression, addiction, and other mental health challenges. These cultures encouraged people to leave their personal problems at home. But mental wellness is not just a personal problem, it is a work-related (and often work-induced) one.

Even companies that have gotten serious about the mental wellbeing of their employees are still playing catch-up. According to a recent WTW survey, while 86% of employers said that mental health, stress, and burnout are top priorities, nearly half (49%) had not formally articulated a wellbeing strategy for their workforce.

Mental health issues remain shrouded in stigma, so it is not enough to merely offer programs. The onus is on leaders to lead by example and show people it is okay to be their authentic selves. Leaders need to demonstrate that sometimes it is simply okay to not be okay.

We must eliminate the notion that there is something bad or negative about getting help or support for mental and emotional health related issues. It is time to normalize mental health care as many people face difficulties. Discussing emotional and mental wellness challenges should be no different than discussing physical ailments and other health concerns. After all, various health organizations estimate that 25% of us will suffer from major depression in our lives, with workplace issues and working environments being among the chief causes. This is an unacceptable legacy of how we work and the workplace environments we have accepted as tolerable.

Here are some eye-opening research results:

> A recent survey from SHRM found that although over 90% of HR professionals think offering mental-health resources can improve the overall health of their workers, only one-third admitted that these resources are a "high priority" for their organizations.

A recent report from Talkspace and Harris Poll confirms that follow-through matters: two out of every three U.S. employees considering leaving their jobs agreed that their employer had not come through on their early pandemic promises to focus on mental health.

In the LinkedIn Global Talent Trends 2022 report, 66% of Gen Z say more investment in mental health will improve company culture. That same report also revealed that 63% of professionals rank work-life balance as the top priority when picking a new job.

An encouraging sign that things in the workplace are shifting in the right direction comes from a survey of 650 workers in Australia. It found that Gen Z workers were the most likely to take a mental health day (48%), followed closely by Millennials at 41%. This bodes well for the future of the workplace. Unfortunately, older workers are not as quick to adapt to this trend, with only 28% of Gen X and a woefully low 13% of Baby Boomers taking mental health days. Thank goodness the younger generations are starting to tear down the taboos around mental health.

More employers need to learn the importance of investing in and supporting a mentally healthy workplace. Leaders have individual responsibility for looking after the wellbeing of their team members. Especially if there is no organization-wide Wellness Culture in place. One best practice: instead of asking the pro forma question "how are you," ask:

Have there been any changes in how you are feeling?

How would you like tomorrow to be different?

What made you smile today?

When did you last feel appreciated or understood?

What has improved for you today?

What has been hardest for you this week?

What are you most excited about this week?

What are you dreading most this week?

What did you do to take care of yourself today?

What do you wish you did a little less of today (or not at all)?

What do you wish you could do more of today (and tomorrow)?

Leadership Wellbeing

Leaders utilizing self-care to improve their overall wellbeing is the precursor to workplace wellness. Leaders need to walk the talk and role model wellbeing, not just talk about wellness. Leaders should set good examples for their teams by bringing positive energy into the workplace and willingly sharing their personal examples of resilience, mental wellness habits, stress management techniques, and overall wellness strategies.

Critically, leaders must understand that sleep is not a luxury. Research has proven a direct link between leading effectively and getting enough sleep. The research also shows that sleep-deprived leaders are less inspiring and motivating. While it used to be a badge of honor to brag about sleeping only a few hours a night, that is false hero talk. In fact, sufficient and restorative sleep should be sacrosanct for leaders.

Additionally, there is no doubt a greater need than ever before for leaders and team members to incorporate mental refresher breaks into the work day. It is important to disconnect from the working world and our electronic devices both in and outside the workplace.

There is absolutely nothing wrong – and a whole lot right – about taking the occasional mental health day. This is more than just taking a day off to relax. It is a strategical and proactive need to unplug from the things, people, and events causing your stress sensors to overwhelm and negatively impact your mindsets, attitudes, thoughts, and behaviors. These should be no-questions-asked days tailored for your self-care and overall mental, physical, and emotional wellbeing.

Signs that you may need a mental health day include the inability to stop thinking about work, feeling like everything at work is a priority, and having a workload that seems overwhelming and never-ending. Other signs include poor sleep, a sense of being less sharp or productive when working, and excessively handling work-related emails and text messages in your so-called after-hours.

Whatever requires your attention also demands your energy. You cannot create anything if you are coming from a place of stress, worry, or anxiety. No one can be stressed and grateful at the same time. How you do one thing is how you do many things. Change your autopilot and change what you do.

Putting on a brave face to project resiliency and strength is not the way to lead. Bosses need to demonstrate self-care. Show and share your vulnerability. Let others know that you face similar emotional stresses and challenges as your direct reports and colleagues. Taking a mental health day is not a sign of weakness or incompetency.

Wellness may be the most beneficial investment you can make in your workforce.

Do Not Forget Self Compassion and Self Care

As a leader, you have to ensure that you do not allow yourself to become drained by taking on other people's issues, problems, and pains. That is neither compassionate nor empathetic leadership. Your role as a leader is to help and guide others through their negative emotional states, not be so empathetic you take on their problems or their emotions.

Being overly empathetic can result in fatigue, stress, anxiety, sadness, gloom, and even despondency. As a leader, you must care for yourself first. Much like the airline safety message of putting on your own oxygen mask first before helping others, prioritizing your self-care and self-empathy is a must.

After all, draining yourself – whether through overworking or being overly empathetic to the emotions and concerns of others – does not set a good example for those you lead or work with. As the saying goes, you cannot pour from an empty cup.

If you are fatigued, anxious, stressed, or emotionally hijacked, you will not be well-positioned to have empathy or express compassion for others. In fact, you are more likely to be insensitive with your words, actions, and behaviors. You are also more likely to be seen as indifferent to the emotions and concerns of others. Understandably, insensitivity and indifference negatively impact relationships, loyalty, and trust.

A crucial aspect of self-care for leaders is defining success on your own terms and criteria. What are your core values, life themes, and belief systems? What brings harmony into your life? These answers are your North Star and provide you guidance when evaluating work/life options and trade-offs.

Your beliefs and values dictate how you operate in life and as a leader. The more congruence in your daily life habits, actions, behaviors, and thoughts with your beliefs and values, the greater will be your wellbeing. Higher congruence creates greater feelings of success and satisfaction.

Almost everything will work again
if you unplug it for a few minutes...
including you.
Anne Lamott

CHAPTER 11

Cooperative Collaboration

Some attributes of leadership are universal
and are often about finding ways of encouraging people
to combine their efforts, their talents, their insights,
their enthusiasm, and their inspiration to work together.
Queen Elizabeth II

We have gone from a business world where the firm with the best and smartest employees wins to one in which the organizations with the greatest collaboration skills win.

Most collaboration in the workplace is forced collaboration. Individuals and teams are thrown together to produce a dictated outcome. So naturally, self-preservation and competition kick in. Who is going to get the credit? Whose idea will win? What is my role? Do I have to contribute or only be seen as contributing? Will this be a waste of my time?

In the pursuit of productivity, individual work roles have become increasingly focused and specialized. The result has been functional silos, isolation, and too much waiting for another person – in another silo – to make a decision or to collaborate.

Plus, annual reviews and salary systems are not built around collaboration. I once had a senior VP in a technology company tell me, "*I will collaborate with anyone from January through August.*" When I asked him why only those eight months, he replied honestly, "*because my annual bonus is based solely on my individual goals, and thus I make sure these objectives are completed by year end.*" At least he was forthright in his response. He knew the company's system and based his priorities on playing within that system.

Mandated and forced collaboration works on dictated objectives and outputs. Cooperative collaboration creates value-added outcomes. Cooperative collaboration encourages buy-in and is based on the knowledge that a rising tide raises all boats. When the culture rewards collaboration, cooperative collaboration is based on:

- Hearts and minds producing ideas and solutions
- Knowing how collaborators contribute value
- Supporters and evangelists advocate for the project or change initiative

Leaders need to nurture, not mandate, collaboration. Doing so turns forced collaboration into cooperative collaboration. When people put their hearts and minds into collaboration, they automatically bring and deploy their best thinking and passions. Ideation and innovation ensue. And they passionately support the project goals and the contributions of others.

Cooperative collaboration ensues with ease, grace, and speed when you change the status quo into the status flow. Rather than the friction, grind, weight, and stress of forced collaboration, you create frictionless and effortless collaboration, which in turn produces creativity, innovation, ideas, and optimal outcomes.

The personal desire to cooperate, combined with the positive emotional energy of being part of a cooperative work group, keeps the brain's working memory stimulated, even while doing other tasks away from the workplace.

People want to contribute. It is part of our human nature. Unfortunately, workplace climates over the past few decades have diminished this human tendency and created the "it's not my job" attitude amongst too much of the workforce. Forced collaboration has instilled a reluctance to contribute more than the bare minimum required to avoid punishment, poor performance reviews, or being cast as "not a team player."

The best way to nurture collaboration is to focus on the people aspect of collaboration, not the task-driven aspects. Remember, team members want collaborating colleagues who:

> They feel good working with
>
> Will treat them with respect
>
> Enable and encourage them to make a contribution
>
> Help them feel personally fulfilled
>
> See the value in the work they do and the contributions (ideas) they make
>
> Ensure everyone thrives individually and collectively

Hearts and Minds

When someone willingly collaborates with others on a task or project, they put their heart and mind into action. This is another way of saying they bring their mental and emotional passion and energy to the task at hand.

In forced collaboration situations, people tend to bring the bare minimum required. They do what is asked of them, often reluctantly. And, unless they see the opportunity for a return or benefit to themselves, they keep their best ideas and solutions hidden. There is no sense in sharing a good idea if no reward or advantage is to be personally gained. Even worse, no one wants to share a good idea that might be stolen and claimed by someone else, particularly their boss.

In contrast, when cooperative collaboration arises, everyone involved shares their ideas and thoughts. This is especially true when leaders have created a psychologically safe environment where team members are unafraid to express their thoughts and ideas.

Additionally, when people are happy to cooperate and fully engage in designing solutions or uncovering opportunities, their brains do not stop working at the end of every project session. Instead, their subconscious brains continue to contemplate options and seek relevant information, even when the individual is not purposefully thinking about the project. Hence, great ideas or thoughts about the project pop up at surprising times, such as in the shower, while driving, or just before falling asleep.

After years of research on what makes teams effective, Google identified a single factor as most important: psychological safety. According to Google, "teammates feel safe to take risks around their team members in a team with high psychological safety. They feel confident that no one on the team will embarrass or punish anyone else for admitting a mistake, asking a question, or offering a new idea." Workplaces infused with psychological safety are safe spaces to learn, fail, experiment, and share the lessons emanating from these endeavors.

As Jack Welch pointed out, "*When people make mistakes, the last thing they need is discipline. It is time for encouragement and confidence building. The job at this point is to restore self-confidence. I think piling on when someone is down is one of the worst things any of us can do.*"

As I tell my clients, permit people to make mistakes. But also hand them the obligation to learn from their errors. That is accountability.

In many ways, psychological safety is also a fancy phrase for trust. When trust is paramount and observable, people feel safe. When trust is combined with enabling people to contribute and add value to discussions and decisions, a powder keg of cooperation ignites.

Advocates and Evangelists

When people work cooperatively and collaboratively with others on a project, their engagement naturally increases. That is an obvious no-brainer.

What is not often anticipated, but usually happens, is that these highly engaged individuals also become enthusiastic advocates for the group and the project objectives.

Their enthusiasm can be contagious, helping lift other team members' spirits and commitment. They bring an optimistic glow to discussions, seeking to turn perceived obstacles into opportunities and ensuring all problems have identified resolutions.

This enthusiasm and positivity spill over outside the workgroup, making them great recruiters for obtaining new team members. They also advocate the benefits of the project to others in the organization. Their evangelistic tendencies promote the project within and across the organization.

Here is a way of evaluating whether your team members work together collaboratively or reluctantly. I call this the Collaboration Continuum, with seven stages running from forced collaboration to evangelistic support:

> Forced collaboration
>
> Reluctance
>
> Uncommitted (but willing to give it a try)
>
> Waiting to see what's in it for me (WIIFM)
>
> Committed
>
> Advocate
>
> Evangelist

This Collaboration Continuum can be used to evaluate individuals, project teams, or the collaboration between cross-functional departments.

Forced collaboration usually starts in the Reluctance to WIIFM range, one reason why so few projects attain full, cooperative collaboration from all participants.

A word of caution: do not attempt to move anyone more than one step along the continuum at a time. It is nearly impossible to turn a WIIFM person directly into an Advocate. Rather, work with such an on-the-fence person to first get them to the Committed stage. After they see the program's benefits more clearly, you can coach them into being an Advocate.

The same goes for the Reluctant participant. All the rah-rah and motivational techniques in the world will not magically turn them into a Committed (or even a WIIFM) participant. Instead, coach and mentor them to the Uncommitted but willing to give it a try stage. Let them experience working with others without the negativity of reluctance and being forced to collaborate. Convince them to give it a try and see how things work out.

You may need to do a bit of micromanaging here. Not quite holding their hand, but staying in constant close contact to see how they are feeling and helping to fend off any situations that might cause them to slip back into reluctance mode. Yes, this takes time and the kind of tenacity to leading people discussed in an earlier chapter!

Personally, I rarely try to move someone from the Advocate level to being an Evangelist. I find that those who become the best evangelists are highly self-motivated and thus do not need prompting or encouragement from me. Their own passion and enthusiasm will bubble up without any influence or suggestions from me.

Moving individuals in your group up the Collaboration Continuum will greatly reduce the feelings of forced collaboration and the associated negative attitudes that this brings. Doing so is probably one of the easiest and most impactful ways to encourage and create workplace harmony for the people you lead.

The Hollywood Approach

Permanent teams reporting to a single functional boss is another anachronism of the pre-pandemic workplace.

While there is much to be disdained about Hollywood's entertainment products and morals, a methodology of cooperative collaboration and adaptability used in the entertainment industry is highly applicable to the business world. It is a structure for producing movies, television programs, and music that more organizations should mimic.

When a project in Hollywood gets funding, a producer (or producers) puts together a team of collaborators who have the single purpose of creating the project (a movie, TV series, pilot program, music album, etc.). For a film, the team comprises a director, actors and actresses, camera crews, set and costume designers, gaffers, stage and sound squads, scriptwriters, and contract vendors such as catering, security, and publicists.

All are specialists in their respective roles and responsibilities. And all are codependent on each other. They come together to collaborate on this one project and then disband when the film is completed. There is no permanency in their professional relationships. They may or may not ever work together again.

However, they are committed to creating this project and working cooperatively together. That is not to say there are never any conflicts or personal agendas. Of course not. But for the most part, the collaboration is cooperative because those on the production team want to be included and see the project finished.

Plus, if they are good at their jobs and are seen as collaborative team players, they are more likely to get hired the next time the producer has funding for her or his subsequent project. Or their reputations will precede them, and other producers and directors will seek them out to be part of their production teams.

Agile businesses will adopt this approach. This methodology's built-in adaptability and flexibility enable leaders to put together teams comprising the most suitable talents who *want* to be on the team. This is a much better approach than forcing a group of available employees to form, storm, norm, and try to perform together.

I used this approach very successfully for seven consecutive years. One of my annual projects was to produce the yearly MasterCard Asia/Pacific regional conference, attended by executives and managers from the financial institutions issuing MasterCard credit and debit cards and other payments industry executives.

Each year I put together a team that worked on creating and organizing this four-day event, which had between 800 and 1400 attendees. The event was held each year in a different city and country, meaning I had to put together a core team along with local suppliers and individuals.

My core team comprised a staging and production company in Manila and three individuals based in Singapore. We would work feverishly together for roughly five months each year, disband, and then regroup each subsequent year (with different local vendors and suppliers each time). In between these gigs, we each went our separate ways and worked on other projects.

Leaders must also become adept at leading remote collaboration. After all, remote working and leading non-co-located employees are definite components of the future of work.

"Every company should accept that, for a certain part of the organization, work from anywhere will be the reality of our lives. What is important is that we are organizing it in a way that the face-to-face collaboration and the connection to the culture of the organization is not lost," says Christian Ulbrich, president and CEO of Jones Lang LaSalle.

Successful remote collaboration is more about people than technology. Technology applications (Teams, Slack, Google Docs, etc.) are tools. Focus on how people like to work together, not force them into adapting to technology. Make the technology adapt to them.

Outputs vs. Outcomes

To propel cooperative collaboration, focus on outcomes instead of outputs. Doing so inherently increases the value contributions of those you want to work together collaboratively.

Giving people or teams a checklist of deliverables for a project or task assignment is neither motivational nor an opportunity for them to provide value. The recipients of a list of outputs to produce do not feel empowered or engaged. Cooperation with others is obligatory and forced because the boss (or management) wants this done. Few people wake up in the morning excited to work on a checklist of output items mandated by their boss or upper management. Such assignments should be for low-value activities which can be quickly accomplished.

On the other hand, if you want collaborative efforts to produce something of value, you are much better off depicting a desired outcome or direction to your team members and then stepping aside. Let them be empowered to create solutions and value. After all, you hired them for their minds, thinking abilities, and creativity. Do not tie their hands and demotivate them with a list of specific deliverables.

Remember, value is in the eyes of the customer, whether this is an internal or external customer. Value comes in many forms, most of which are not monetary in nature. Value can be described in terms of time savings, heightened customer experiences, increased convenience, and many other ways.

On straightforward implementation tasks, a checklist of outputs may be desirable. But understand that this will not necessarily lead to high levels of cooperation and collaboration. On the other hand, when innovation, creativity, and stupendous problem solving are required or desirable, you want to provide opportunities for value generation by empowering your teams to focus on outcomes, not outputs.

An example from my career happened when I was the Marketing VP of a major U.S. bank in Asia. We were launching a new deposit product and needed a customer statement showing the amount deposited and tenure. This was a straightforward task for our IT department. The output was simple: a monthly statement showing the amount deposited, the date of deposit, and the date that the deposit was eligible for rollover (renewal). They delivered exactly what I requested with no value added.

Later that year, I challenged the IT department to produce a monthly customer statement that consolidated all the products and services each customer had with us – AND those they did not have. The desired outcome was for us to use the monthly customer statement as a cross-selling piece of marketing communication rather than just a formal monthly financial reporting document.

This time, the IT folks and members of my team – along with the customer service department and our in-house legal staff – all worked collaboratively to create a new and innovative monthly customer statement. While this may seem like a passé example today, trust me, this was innovative thinking back in 1991 (before mobile devices, apps, and even the origins of the Internet!!). We did not have cloud computing back then, only an IBM AS400 mainframe (which I often suspected was held together with rubber bands and duct tape).

You want to make it easy and safe for team members to collaborate cooperatively. The leaders' role is to eliminate or minimize all barriers to cooperative collaboration. In a safe environment, employees can relax, invoking the brain's higher capacity for social engagement, innovation, creativity, and ambition.

Unfortunately, psychological safety is missing in far too many organizations. As a result, self-silencing affects too much of the workplace as people are afraid to speak up and share their thoughts and ideas.

Neuroscience corroborates this point. When the amygdala registers a threat to our safety, we get cut off from the executive function of the prefrontal cortex, inhibiting creativity and the drive for excellence. When the amygdala takes over, we also lose access to the social engagement system of the limbic brain, making people more afraid and less willing to speak up.

From a neuroscience perspective, making sure that people feel safe needs to be a primary focus for leaders. Research has repeatedly shown that empowered teams are more productive, proactive, and better at producing value-added outcomes. Participants on such teams also exhibit higher levels of job satisfaction and commitment to the team and organization.

A leader is best
when people barely know he exists,
when his work is done, his aim fulfilled,
they will say:
we did it ourselves.
Lao-Tzu

CHAPTER 12

Lifelong Learning

They know enough who know how to learn.
Henry Adams

One of my favorite and most repeated mantras is: Never stop learning because life never stops teaching.

The leadership dinosaurs of the post-pandemic period will be those who cannot learn, unlearn, and relearn. The same can be said for organizations, both large and small.

Lifelong learning is a wonderful mindset. Over the past 30 years, I have mentored, coached, and trained over 10,000 leaders from every part of the world. Yet I still read 35-45 articles each month on leadership, leadership skills, employee engagement, decision making, and other relevant topics. And each year, I read up to a dozen books on leadership.

A lifelong learning mentality is a component of a growth mindset. What is a mindset? A mindset is a self-referential theory that we each hold about our own intelligence and that of others.

If we believe intelligence is pretty much set early in life and unchangeable, this is called a Fixed Mindset. If we believe that intelligence is fluid and variable depending on effort, learning, and experience, then this is called a Growth Mindset.

Fixed Mindset people tend to believe that their personal qualities (such as intelligence and other personality traits) are set in stone from a very early age. You are basically who you are with innate levels of intelligence and ability that do not change or alter only slightly. This is a core belief that a person's raw intellect is mainly fixed and not something that can be evolved, enhanced, or developed.

Taking your self-image too seriously is also a symptom of a fixed mindset. It keeps you mentally stuck and prohibits growth. Thinking of yourself as "a marketing person" or a "financial controller" can keep you stagnant and block personal growth. Drop the labels and the limitations around your self-image and a world of opportunity will open to you.

On the other hand, those with a Growth Mindset believe that effort, education, learning, and training can transform a person's qualities and traits, including their intelligence. In this mindset, you tend to believe that raw intellect can evolve with focus, application, and effort. You will also tend to believe that a lack of understanding or knowledge of any subject is merely a prompt to dig deeper or try harder.

You cannot be a Humony Leader with a Fixed Mindset. Humony Leaders place high importance on continually developing themselves and the people they lead. This comes through formal learning opportunities, experiences, and insights from others.

It is highly recommended that you cultivate a growth mindset throughout your team and, eventually, throughout the organization. Fortunately, a growth mindset can be learned, though it takes a mindset change combined with effort and tenacity. For instance, despite living most of my adult life outside the United States, I longed told myself and others that I had no capability to learn a second language. I am not good at languages was my go-to mantra. A year ago, I eliminated that mental manacle with new thinking and today I am learning Spanish.

As famed psychologist Abraham Maslow noted decades ago, *"One can choose to go back toward safety or forward toward growth. Growth must be chosen again and again; fear must be overcome again and again."*

A growth mindset is a strong internal compass pointing to your ability to control and create a positive way forward whenever inevitable mistakes and missteps occur. A static mindset does not learn from setbacks, avoids risk, and is apathetic toward trying new things.

Leaders (and employees) need to take responsibility for their own development. But to do so, they must engage a growth mindset and put aside their fixed mindsets.

With a growth mindset, your internal chatter changes significantly. Examples are:

I give up. >>> I will try something different.

I failed. >>> Mistakes help me learn / I have learned from that mistake.

I will never be smart enough. >>> I will learn how

to do this.

I am not good at this. >>> This may take me some time.

This is too hard. >>> What am I missing?

I cannot do this. >>> I do not know how to do this yet.

Lastly, please remember that continuous training of your team members, especially in the "soft skills" areas of teamwork, collaboration, and working across boundaries, is the key to scaling every part of your business.

Lifelong Learning

Everyone, particularly people leaders, must embrace lifelong learning as a necessity, not a luxury.

The most important skill people need to develop is "learning agility." Learning agility is having the curiosity and motivation to learn new things through a multitude of channels throughout the entirety of your career (and your life).

Gone are the days when a four-year degree provides you with all the knowledge you need to stay competitive in your professional career. What you learned in college should be considered part of your ongoing process of self-improvement, not the end goal of your education.

Learning agility and having a growth mindset are closely interlinked and necessary in a world where the skills we need change faster than ever and our need to learn new material, techniques, and methods is ever rising.

The number one need for employees (and even contract workers, consultants, and entrepreneurs) is to remain relevant and hirable in a world of uncertainty.

As Steve Cadigan, author of *Workquake*, points out, *"Employability is the new job security."* Humony Leadership skills make you more employable, especially the ability to manage and adapt to uncertainty and ambiguity. People need to develop a proactive, take-charge approach to education and training that extends into everyday life, not just in classrooms and offices.

The best personal competitive advantage you can develop is the capacity to grow, learn, and adapt. Thus, you will be prepared to succeed regardless of how markets or technology change. Your ability to learn skills, not the skills themselves, will allow you to weather any career change. This is the ultimate career insurance.

Experience should not hold you back from learning and seeing opportunities from change. Yet too often, it is. Established thinking patterns and mindsets, combined with success in the pre-pandemic world, shut off receiving new information. Many of us need to unlearn old and established methods of doing and thinking to remain relevant in today's shifting world.

Smart companies are starting to focus on learning agility: what did you learn and how fast did you successfully apply it? Employers will increasingly desire people who can change, adapt, and grow because that is the reality of the business world today.

Unfortunately, too many companies continue to prepare for the future with obsolete business models. A start-up offers greater flexibility, a lack of bureaucracy, and more meaningful work. So how do you create a start-up climate in your organization? Focus on those three elements: change, adapt, and grow.

Today, more than 25% of the working population undergoes a career transition yearly. Half of all hourly workers leave new jobs within the first 120 days, according to research conducted for the SHRM Foundation by Talya N. Bauerm, a professor of management at Portland State University.

As I wrote in the Introduction, the skills of the future are not technical; they are behavioral. These skills are not "soft." Rather, they are highly complex, continuously changing, and often take months to inculcate into individual mindsets and behaviors.

Leadership success will come via learning adaptability, frequency, agility, and velocity.

Leading Self Development

Understanding the importance of self-awareness and self-understanding in developing one's leadership mindsets and skills is imperative. These two qualities are equally important when it comes to your own self-development. For, as philosopher Baltasar Gracián wrote, *"Self-correction begins with self-knowledge."*

Learning to lead yourself and your professional development reveals your values, non-negotiables, principles, and interests. This gives you direction and boundaries that will help keep you on course. It also keeps you from leading people and teams to places you do not want to go or with methods you do not want to use.

Constantly thinking about and exploring the foundation of your leadership philosophy and mindset is also a core component of your ongoing leadership development journey.

Think about it. Integrity, communicating, coaching, listening, providing feedback, delegation, influencing, motivating, and decision making may be called "soft skills." However, they are the very skills you need to develop and grow as a leader. You do not want your team members to have only the same skills in three years as they do now. For the same reasons, you cannot afford to have only the same skills, capabilities, and competencies three years from now as you do today.

Additionally, as a leader, you are in charge of your self-development. You cannot afford to wait around for the talent development department or human resources folks, or even your manager, to create leadership development opportunities for you. When this does happen, take full advantage of such opportunities. But do not wait for such occasions to arise. Passivity is not an option. Neither is relying on your organization or your manager (unless she or he is a Humony Leader!).

No leader should wait around for their manager to tell them how to develop as a leader. As I once heard April Arnzen, Senior Vice President and Chief People Officer at Micron Technology, tell her senior leaders in this Fortune 500 organization, *"Don't ever wait around for someone else to tell you how to develop yourself.*" That is sage advice for leaders at any level of any organization.

The truth is, you will never learn everything you need to know to be a great leader. Continuous learning and development are mandatory for continued leadership success.

The biggest mistake new managers make is thinking they already know everything they need to know to excel in their new leadership role. However, the skills, knowledge, and experiences that create a successful and talented individual contributor are not necessarily transferable to the role of a leader.

For instance, you may know how to motivate yourself. But what motivates you is not necessarily what motivates any or all of your team members. The same applies to communication preferences. You may prefer delivering your messages orally, but some team members may need to see these in writing to understand and retain the information. This advice from Jedi Master Yoda is particularly relevant for both new and experienced leaders, "*You must unlearn what you have learned.*"

All great leaders know that they need to develop themselves continuously. This is why taking charge and leading one's own personal and professional development is a core component of the art of great leadership.

Create habits to be the leader you want to be. To be a people-centric leader, put one-on-one discussions with your team members at the top of your weekly priority list. Spend more time coaching and mentoring your team members than in meetings and discussions with your peers and colleagues. Practice mindfulness techniques at work so that you more often respond than react to situations, people, and events (refer back to the chapter on Wellbeing and Stress Management for tips).

Creating a Learning and Growth Mindset Culture

Psychological safety is one of the pillars of a learning culture within an organization. This includes making it safe for people to express ideas and learn from mistakes without fear of punishment or embarrassment.

When such psychological safety is in place, people are more willing to admit to their errors, figure out how to rectify these, and learn how to prevent the replication or repetition of their mistakes. Even more important, they are willing to share the lessons learned from their blunders and bungles throughout the organization, thus helping to prevent the replication or repetition by others. This is a true learning culture.

Another benefit: you start to create a growth mindset throughout your team and, eventually, throughout the organization. Recognizing mistakes and shortcomings, while not pleasant, need not be painful if the right culture is in place. Everyone makes mistakes at some point. Often the best lessons come via slipups and miscalculations.

So, part of a Growth Mindset Culture is the willingness to learn from mistakes. But, of course, you have to create a psychologically safe environment within your team for this to happen.

In cultures of punishment and fear, mistakes are swept under the carpet and hidden. Hence, any lessons are ignored or kept secret. In a culture of learning, the lessons are given priority and precedence over the errors made.

Likewise, in a performance-focused culture, people are held accountable only for results. In a learning culture, people are held accountable for results and the lessons learned applicable to future progress. In a performance culture, personal success is built on continuously proving yourself by delivering results. In a learning culture, personal success comes through improving yourself and others, leading to continuous improvement of the organization.

Organizations with learning cultures grow and expand more rapidly and extensively than those with performance cultures. After all, some results are attained through luck and the fortunes of the market moving in the right direction and at the right pace. But such successes are not repeatable, leading to many one-hit wonders.

Many of the most successful companies today, like Amazon, Apple, and Google, have experienced numerous product and market failures. But these companies treat their failures like experiments, enabling them to apply and leverage the lessons learned into future sustainable successes.

Employees who are trained and feel they are growing are more likely to stay, reducing employee attrition costs. Also, they become more experienced and higher producers. Another pair of virtuous cycles.

Guess what? Meeting goals and objectives with less time, energy, and effort provides more time for learning and development, coaching, and mentoring. Better equipped staff thus go on to produce higher quality results. Perhaps the best virtuous cycle of all!

Leadership Development Shortfalls
Where do leaders first learn their leadership skills?

Usually, this comes from two sources: a) the leadership behaviors and actions of the bosses they have had throughout the various stages of their careers, and b) being thrown into the front lines of leadership with little more than expressions of confidence and best wishes by their managers.

Unfortunately, great individual contributors do not necessarily make good managers or great leaders. When promoted into supervisory or managerial roles, they tend to focus on the managerial aspects of processes, procedures, reporting, and executing what they are told.

As a result, they are unprepared for the critical people leadership skills of coaching, providing feedback, increasing employee engagement, motivating team members, developing people, delegating, obtaining buy-in and commitment, fueling innovation, and generating new ideas.

Transitioning from a successful individual contributor role into a supervisory or manager position is fraught with challenges, concerns, and worries. This is a profound change with high risks of failure, personal dissatisfaction, team disenchantment, and even team member disengagement.

In many organizations, training primarily focuses on developing technical skills — creating managers and individual contributors who are functionally knowledgeable and competent in their respective jobs but are not trained in the fundamentals of leading people.

One area of particular weakness in mid-level leaders and new supervisors that I have noticed in my 30 years of international leadership development is their inability to give relevant, useful, and beneficial feedback. This inexperience and lack of expertise in proper feedback methodology significantly handicaps their ability to lead other team members.

Periods of high revenue growth often mask shortcomings in talent development, particularly within fast-growing small businesses and privately-owned companies. Gaps in existing leadership skills and competencies tend to go unnoticed when revenue rapidly increases yearly. It is only when growth suddenly declines that company owners and senior leaders become acutely aware of the significant shortfalls in leadership talent throughout the organization that are creating bottlenecks to continued growth.

Our best advice: do not let these leadership development shortfalls happen to you. Take charge of your own leadership development.

Your Leadership Development

Leadership development is a continuous journey. Every great leader is always looking for new leadership ideas, techniques, and methodologies. The art of great leadership requires a continuous evaluation and evolution of one's leadership skills, mindset, philosophy, actions, and development.

While it is important to understand your strengths and gaps, it is an error to focus only on your perceived or known weak areas. Rather, figuring out how to leverage your strengths to close gaps when desired (and hire to fill gaps when not desired) is extremely important. And it is okay to have some gap areas. Hiring to fill gaps in skill areas that are not your strong suit or not in your passionate zone is best. For me, I have no desire to learn how to make graphs and pie charts from Excel. Nor do I want to become super proficient in creating elegant PowerPoint slides. Those are chores best left for people more capable and knowledgeable than me.

No one needs to be a superwoman or superman with all skills and powers. Learning how to learn is better than learning knowledge. This is why the concept of college degrees for entry-level positions is sorely outdated.

Fortunately, like any skill, leadership can be learned. Great leadership is an art based on a core set of skills and behaviors you can learn. And your proficiency in leadership can be improved through continuous practice and utilization of the leadership methods and tools you choose to use.

A key to developing your leadership skills is to monitor your experiences, thoughts, and actions throughout the day. Research reported in *Harvard Business Review* (August 2017) showed that "*leaders who are in learning mode develop stronger leadership skills than their peers.*"

A clear understanding of the current levels of one's various leadership skills is also critically important. But this does not mean you should be overly critical of your current skill levels or any mistakes you make. It is far better to interpret a setback as evidence that you have not yet developed expertise in a particular skill than to allow a setback to convince you that you are not cut out to be a leader.

Three tips for building your leadership skills:

1) Focus on improvement over perfection. Do not lose sight of improvement by trying to become perfect at a particular skill. And give yourself credit when you have made improvements, even while knowing you still have room to improve.

2) Focus on process over results. One of my favorite pieces of advice to leaders applies to your development efforts: recognize effort and reward results. Keep your focus on the process of implementing a new skill and the results will come.

3) Focus on the positives over the negatives. We all tend to focus on what we need to improve while forgetting to leverage the strengths of the skills we already have in place. Do not lose focus on what you are doing well; use these well-honed skills to build your other leadership skills.

By the way, these same three rules apply when helping team members or colleagues develop professionally.

Chances are you already know what leadership gaps you have and what your leadership strengths are. The key to leveraging your strengths is through consistent behavior and actions.

Purposeful action, based on your core leadership beliefs, prevents handling every situation you encounter in an inconsistent, case-by-case manner.

Your leadership strengths can also minimize or close any leadership skill gaps you have. Or at least buy you time to eliminate these gaps through coaching from others, reading and video research, or a formal classroom session.

My last advice is to approach your leadership development and learning journey with an open mind. Learning to lead others can feel enticing, alluring, exciting, and even satisfying. But learning to lead and develop yourself will feel powerful, empowered, aligned, confident, and authentically fulfilled.

No matter where you are within your current (or future) organization, your focus should move from trying to keep your job to ensuring you are constantly developing and growing. This will keep you employable and relatively immune to disruptions and unexpected changes that may force your company to let you go. To stay relevant, you must proactively acquire new knowledge skills and professional networks on an ongoing basis.

Remember, progress in self-development requires reflection, planning, action, and commitment. Repeated continuously.

Also, keep in mind that your continuous development as a leader is your responsibility (as well as your boss's). But if she or he is not developing you, that is no excuse for you to do likewise. Keep at the forefront of your thoughts the quote from April Arnzen of Micron Technology a few pages ago. Never wait for someone else to tell you how to develop yourself or your leadership skills.

There is no valid excuse for any leader for not constantly upgrading their leadership, motivation, communication, collaboration, coaching, and people development skills. You can readily find many free and paid leadership and skill development resources on the Internet. These include articles, videos, book excerpts, workshops, and learning programs. To help you, I have a list of highly recommended leadership development resources on my company website at www.CalienteLeadership.com.

Google has a policy allowing Googlers to spend 20% of their time on any project they think will benefit Google. I coach leaders to apply this concept to themselves and encourage you to do the same. In other words, spend 15% to 20% of your time on self-motivation, skill mastery, or the most important issues facing you and your team members. After all, you cannot improve your skills or create innovative solutions to essential matters sitting in meetings all day long.

How do you reach this 15% level? Start by blocking your calendar. Give yourself six hours per week to work on whatever you want, professionally or personally. Your colleagues – and your boss – must respect this. They cannot call meetings or require your attendance during these periods of do not disturb. The building must be on fire, or the servers must be down, for you to be disturbed.

This frees up to six hours per week to learn and master the critical concerns of you and your team members, such as:

Human, Equality, and Inclusion practices

Workplace Wellness techniques and strategies

Workplace Harmony creation

Individual and team development

Product concepts

Productivity Innovations

Changes to processes or procedures

These are not "one and done" issues where you take action or dictate a new policy after listening to a presentation or discussion. These are issues that need continuous thinking, monitoring, and managing. They are not problems to be resolved. In fact, they are never fully resolved due to the continuous changes in the workplace and society.

Developing Others

Managers often overlook the people development aspect of leadership, especially those put into leadership positions for the first time, such as new supervisors, frontline managers, and newly appointed sales managers who have been promoted due to high sales performance.

Leaders who aim to attract disciples are interested in authority, power, status, and control. They drive to make people get things done — usually their way (or the highway). Their focus is only on creating more high performers for their team. While this often produces wonderful short-term results, it is not a sustainable or replicable leadership methodology. It also tends to contribute to employee burnout and high employee attrition rates.

However, all great leaders know that their mission is not to focus only on short-term team results. Rather, they set out to create more high performers and more good leaders for their organizations, not just their teams. This is why people development is a core component of the art of great leadership and one of the critical aspects of Humony Leadership.

Here is a revealing exercise I run in my leadership development programs and one-on-one mentoring sessions. If you would like to participate, grab a writing instrument and a piece of paper.

The exercise is to answer these three questions while thinking about a typical two-week period at work:

1) What percentage of your time is spent attending meetings, participating in conference calls, or reading/responding/deleting/sending emails?

2) What percentage of your time is spent reviewing work progress or results (this includes reading and reviewing documents or reports) or generating reports or presentations related to work progress or results?

3) What percentage of your time is spent doing Individual Contributor work or work that could be delegated?

Add up the three figures. Is the total higher than 80%? Higher than 90%? Over 100%?

Subtract the total from 100. That is the percent of time remaining for developing your people.

For many leaders, especially mid-level leaders and supervisors, people development time is less than 15%. Yet people development is (or should be) one of the key priorities for all leaders, as it is one of the most important drivers of sustainable success for any organization.

I would suggest that people development should be the single most important priority for all leaders. After all, if great leadership is achieving progress through the involvement and actions of others, then greater progress will be made when the people being led are constantly being developed and improved.

Additionally, people development is a highly leveraged catalyst for individuals and the organization. That is why the best leadership is bringing out the talent in others.

Without growth in the people you lead, growth trajectories for your organization will flatten. Organizational growth rises when the professional and personal capabilities of the human workforce continue to increase. It is that simple.

Do not moan and make excuses like, "what if I develop and train my people and then some of them leave?" Instead, be more concerned about what will happen if you do not develop and train your team members and they stay. How competitive will you be in that situation? Where will your organizational growth come from if your team members are not being developed to handle more complicated and challenging situations?

Yes, some might leave after being trained and developed. But most likely, more will stay. And those who stay will have more competence and confidence. Especially when they realize that these powerful "soft skills" they are learning are also truly formidable life skills.

Actually, it is okay for people to leave the organization if they no longer see a career path for them internally. Having been supported in their growth and development, they will speak highly of their leaders and the organization. They may even partner with you in the future or return with increased skills and experience!

As we come out of the pandemic, employees will long remember how their managers, supervisors, and leaders supported them (or did not support them) during the pandemic years. They will also remember which organizations continued to develop and grow them during the long periods of lockdown and mandatory work-from-home.

Likewise, they will not fondly recall those organizations which nuked training and development programs and those leaders who failed to coach them during this period. While it may be too late to make amends for your individual and organizational actions during the pandemic, the time to take corrective action for your remaining workforce is right now. Starting today.

Developing People and Teams

Developing team members is the moral (and mental) starting point for everything a Humony Leader does. Such leaders value the whole human being of each person they lead, constantly focusing on ways to grow and develop them individually and collectively.

Unfortunately, according to Gallup's research, only 30% of employees believe that their managers and leaders care about their development. If employees are told they have limited choices and their growth is not a priority for the organization, they will leave. This is definitely a time when actions speak louder than words.

One of the most frightful things I read recently was Google executive chairman Eric Schmidt saying, "*I don't know how you build great management virtually.*" Well, he and his colleagues need to learn how to do so immediately! Growing great managers and others virtually is mandatory for the New Abnormal.

Not only is Mr. Schmidt and his team of executives at risk of losing good Google employees, but that mentality will also reduce the company's ability to attract new talent. A McKinsey report in 2021 showed that over 80% of job seekers are specifically looking for work that enables them to grow. At a minimum, Google now looks less attractive to future recruiting candidates, especially those wanting to work remotely while developing their leadership careers.

Not surprisingly, the annual FORTUNE 100 Best Companies to Work For study routinely shows that the best companies are committed to employee development. The companies on this list devoted an average of 65 hours per annum toward developing salaried employees. They also invested an average of 58 hours per year in developing their hourly workers.

Focusing on people development differentiates the best companies to work for from others. Focusing on people development is also one of the characteristics differentiating great leaders from good leaders.

Everyone on your team has talents that can be improved. These can be the functional skills needed to perform their jobs or the interpersonal skills required to get work done in collaboration or cooperation with others. Great leaders ensure that all members of their teams receive ongoing development, both formally and informally.

This is nothing new. For, as John Quincy Adams noted centuries ago, *"If your actions inspire others to dream more, learn more, do more, and become more, you are a leader."* Unfortunately, in recent decades, allowing and enabling leaders to focus on developing the skills of their people has been misplaced by an overemphasis on quarterly profits and other short-term performance measurements.

So how do you go about being an excellent leader of people development?

First, understand that you are accountable for developing the skills of your team members. Your organization's Human Resources and Talent Development departments are resources for you to use in this endeavor. But it is your responsibility to ensure the continuous development of your team members and yourself, not theirs.

Your Human Resources and Talent Development colleagues should take the lead only on formal training events, including classroom and virtual training programs. But even when they do, you remain responsible and accountable for the execution of these programs.

Continuous development of yourself and your people is one of the most important foundational aspects of building a Humony Climate in your workgroup.

The ability to learn
is the most important quality
a leader can have.
Sheryl Sandberg

CHAPTER 13

Creating a Humony Climate. Leading a Humony Culture.

The fact is that people are good.
Give people affection and security,
and they will give affection and be secure
in their feelings and their behavior.
Abraham Maslow

There are many systemic challenges today impacting work and the workplace environment. At the heart of these is a simple fact: work is not working for many people. In fact, work and the workplace, along with the behaviors, actions, and attitudes of too many leaders, have alienated millions of people.

Work is no longer a place or concept nourishing people or enabling them to thrive. Rather, work is often something to withstand and survive. Why? Because the workplace rarely allows or enables the whole human being. Individuals are asking: what is work doing for me? Other than a paycheck, not much.

The pre-pandemic way of working no longer provides an adequate sense of purpose, meaning, importance, or significance. This old workplace model means most of the workforce now needs to find these attributes elsewhere. They need to find valued sources of nourishment, passion, and purpose outside the workplace instead of in their careers. As we have witnessed since the summer of 2021, this leads to significantly higher employee turnover.

The workplace is an activity-rich environment. Act, act, act. Do, do, do. Non-stop action. People are afraid to be seen thinking instead of doing! Yet many have been hired to think, ideate, envisage, create, and innovate. These are value-producing things derived from mental cognition and contemplation, not from activity and commotion.

Leaders need to turn the workplace – in all its forms, including co-location, remote, and hybrid arrangements – into rich, engaging, interactive, and cooperation inducing environments. The workplace needs to have a central nucleus where the main contributions are ideas, thoughts, innovations, challenges to the status quo, insights, and unique perspectives. To enable people to flourish and thrive, the workplace environment must allow every person to bring their full, human selves into their jobs without fear of ridicule, judgment, or humiliation.

In other words, the workplace environment needs to become a place of harmony led by Humony Leaders. Once again, this requires a significant mindset change that will come naturally to Humony Leaders. Such leaders reframe their thinking to focus on the value contributions being made by their team members.

Humony Leaders want people to focus on work outcomes, not work activities. For example, is housekeeping responsible for making beds or pleasing guests? From a customer's perspective – as well as a Humony Leader's standpoint – the answer of pleasing guests is obvious. The same is true for the passionate housekeeper who wants to do more each day than fold bed covers and tuck in sheets.

Repressing people's passion is exhausting. Yet that is what too many managers do by focusing on work activities instead of outcomes. In doing so, they are cutting off the internal energy of their employees and preventing them from attaining flow. People need energy and flow.

I challenge you to ask your employees: do you have a chance to use your strengths every day? Throughout each work day? Were you excited to go to work last week? Typically, only around 17% can honestly reply yes to these questions. Is that their fault? Definitely not. It results from outdated work processes, obsolete organization structures and hierarchies, and a plethora of managers focused only on results and not their people.

Managers and leaders love to hold one-on-one status reviews, mostly for the purpose of information gathering so they can answer any questions from their own managers and leaders. At the core of these sessions is an emphasis on project status, hurdles, obstacles, and the likelihood of deadline achievement. Instead, your number one question as a leader in these discussions should be: "what are your priorities for the week, and what can I do to help?"

Workplace Climate

Whatever size team you lead, you are responsible for the workplace climate of that team. Climate is different from organizational culture, which permeates the entire organization. Culture is top-down driven. It cascades across the entire organization, for good or bad.

A strong corporate culture can even overpower national and societal cultures. When I worked at Citibank in Singapore, 98% of our workforce were Singaporeans. However, they identified more readily with the global Citibank culture than with many aspects of their local culture. Hence, our culture was significantly different than that of the local banks, where the Singaporean culture predominated. For example, the local banks were much more hierarchical in their decision-making processes, typical of most Asian cultures. At Citibank, decisions were unhesitantly pushed down to the manager and AVP levels, with only the most strategic decisions being discussed by the VP leadership team.

On the other hand, the workplace climate is driven by the managers and leaders of each workgroup. Even in organizations with stellar corporate cultures, there will be dozens, even hundreds, of different workplace climates. For instance, one department head may be exceedingly friendly and outgoing, while another is surly and best described as a taskmaster. Or one leader may be known for constantly expressing gratitude and appreciation to her or his team members for their efforts. At the same time, another could have the attitude that staff are well paid, are expected to perform well, and thus do not need to be praised or acknowledged.

There are many types of leaders and managers and a wide variety can be found in every organization. This is why the adage that people leave bosses, not organizations, rings so true. Those bosses create intolerable workplace climates even in organizations with celebrated corporate cultures.

The workplace climate is the area under your leadership dominion. It is how it feels to work for you and be on your team. To be a Humony Leader, you will want the nucleus of your workplace climate centered on four interlocking elements:

People Come First

Trust

Decision Making and Buy-In

Psychological Safety Leads to Harmony

One silver lining from the pandemic is that this is the perfect opportunity to reconstruct and realign your workplace climate. In many ways, every organization is a new organization. The past two years have been highly interruptive. And no one is returning 100% to the pre-pandemic ways of working, collaborating, and producing.

Since you have to create and construct these new ways anyway, you will be best off doing so with a Humony Leadership perspective and mindset. Even if creating a Humony Climate is only for the team you lead. Of course, greater results will arise if a Humony Culture is implemented across departments, SBUs, and entire organizations.

A key ingredient of Humony Leadership climates and cultures is openness and transparency. Leaders must be willing to acknowledge and share when their struggles, doubts, and concerns overlap with those of their team members. We do not need stoic, uncaring, heartless leaders anymore. These are not characteristics of true strength.

Strong leaders are those who share their stories of resilience and adaptability. Strong leaders admit they do not have all the answers or solutions. Strong leaders know they need to continue learning, not rest on past successes or laurels.

Leaders are vital to the performance of their teams. However, many leaders, particularly first-time supervisors, managers, and team leaders, are undertrained, uninspired, over-stretched, and under-supported. Yet, they are the keyholders best positioned to unlock the performance of every organization's most important resource: the human talent.

It is time to remove the shackles of the past and eliminate autonomic behaviors no longer suited for today's environment. Autonomic behaviors are not productive if they are rooted in the past.

This requires a people-centered approach at all levels. For everyone who leads people. It will become the ecosystem for your organization or team. A Humony Leadership Culture ecosystem.

People Come First

Richard Branson showed he understood this when he said: *"Employees come first. If you take care of your employees, they will take care of the clients.*" Howard Schultz had a similar philosophy while building Starbucks across the globe: "*You cannot create long-term value for the shareholder unless you create long-term value for the employees and the communities you serve.*"

For Humony Leaders, you will want to replace the word "employees" with "people" in the two quotes in the above paragraph. This is a mindset change and helps to prevent you from falling into old, bad habits of thinking of those you lead as staff, resources, and all the other acronyms used to label the paid workforce. Stick to *humans* and *people;* your approach to leading them will differ for the better. As you have probably noticed, I often use "team members" in this book as I find this term less degrading than the terms employees, staff, human resources, and human capital.

Leaders need to prepare for a long period of prioritizing the humanity of the workplace and the people who work with and for them. Your results will depend on this. As will your leadership reputation and legacy. Let me be blunt about the "what's in it for me" facet of Humony Leadership. Even if others in your organization do not become Humony Leaders, the success of your team – and your personal career success – will be enhanced and assured by becoming a Humony Leader.

Team members will long remember – and either rant or rave about – how well their leaders and managers supported them, or did not, during these post-pandemic years and beyond. Without a doubt, those leaders who do not adjust to the new reality of leadership will crumble and see their careers plateau.

The same will be true for organizations that do not establish corporate cultures better suited for today's times.

Interestingly, a people-centered approach helps foster innovation. A study by Texas A&M University researchers found that people feel safer trying out new ideas and taking calculated risks when they feel their leaders and managers are empathetic. By instilling a feeling of psychological safety within the workplace climate, leaders establish an environment where team members know they will not be shamed and blamed when things go astray. As a result, they feel safer sharing thoughts and trying new ideas. This leads to increased innovation, productivity, and results.

Drop the concepts of Human Capital and employees as resources. These labels place employees on the same level as equipment, plants, buildings, raw materials, and other non-sentient assets.

Let me also re-emphasize what I wrote at the beginning of this book. This is about putting people first, not instead of results and profits. Putting people first means making it a priority to consider the people aspects – and the people costs – of decisions and actions.

Please do not confuse "people costs" with payroll and employee benefit programs. This is not at all what I mean. The people cost I am citing is the toll and impact on your people and your workplace climate resulting from your leadership decisions and actions. Before you make a final decision or initiate action, you should evaluate how these will impact the stress and health of your people and the harmony of your workplace climate. Think of these issues in terms of both short-term impact and long-term consequences.

You should also evaluate if your people have the right tools, resources, and experience to execute to your desired standards. Likewise, do they have the right skills or the requisite development opportunity available to close any skill gaps? If not, these insufficiencies will undoubtedly cause negative stress and anxiety, thus leading to less-than-optimal performance.

Are such evaluations limiting? Only if you allow the inadequacies and deficiencies to remain as hurdles and obstacles. Identifying these gaps and shortages up front creates the opportunity to close them. Or to become more innovative in your thinking.

Trust

Trust is the foundational element of leadership and a Humony Culture. Without trust, nothing else a leader does or says matters. It is like oxygen, the foundational element of life. If you put an animal or a plant in a glass container and seal it tight, the oxygen evaporates and the animal or plant dies. The same with trust. If it evaporates, leadership dies.

Trust is not something you are automatically granted as a leader. For leaders, trust has to be earned and maintained. You can best earn the trust of the people you lead by trusting them first. I once had a new manager tell our team on his first day, "here are the ways you can earn my trust." That might have worked in the 1990s. It will not work today. You are better off stating, "You each have my trust. Here are the ways you can lose this trust."

Trust first and you will receive trust in return. Start by not trusting others and what you will receive back is a lack of trust in you.

The pre-pandemic hierarchical structure of the boss representing "management" and driving their teams through intimidation, micromanaging, fear, power politics, and control was dysfunctional. One of the first lessons of the pandemic lockdowns: it is nearly impossible to manage by fear from a distance. As the lockdowns continued, power and control by such managers was eroded and all but lost.

Meanwhile, teams with trusted leaders flourished and thrived during the pandemic. In fact, in many ways, these teams got stronger as long as their leaders exhibited trust in their team members. When trust was prevalent, employees continued to produce results while working from home. When trust was absent or declined, the desire to skive, shirk responsibilities, and start working side hustles increased.

Without trust, minimal creativity and productivity are displayed by the workforce. The lack of trust ensures minimal effort and a focus by employees on self-protection over collaboration and sharing.

Sadly, some organizations demonstrate their lack of trust in employees by monitoring their keyboard and computer activity when they work from home. This is disgusting and an abhorrent practice. Fortunately, some government entities are stepping in to prevent this. A New York State law has already banned such digital surveillance. I am sure it will be the first of many such legislative actions.

Decision Making and Buy-In

Victor Frankl wrote there is a space between a stimulus and a response; in that space, you have the freedom to choose to react or respond.

This is the space you want to seek. This is the space to incorporate into a Humony Culture. In this space, Humony Leaders will pause to ask questions, review alternative courses of action, consider options, and then make a rationally based decision instead of an emotionally induced one. In doing so, you get yourself off autopilot, out of reaction mode, and into a rational response approach.

The other benefit to your decision-making processes from being a Humony Leader is that you will be more inclusive when making decisions, especially regarding decisions on implementation actions, goals, and measurements. Greater diversity of thought and input results in increased odds for creativity, innovation, and optimal solutions.

Plus, as discussed in the chapter on adaptability, leaders can be best prepared to move quickly by having multifaceted options and plans ready before circumstances dictate the need to pivot or alter action.

Lastly, as mentioned several times, by putting people first, you will make better decisions for those you lead, your organization, and the communities in which you operate. Before any decision is finalized, always ask:

What will be the cost and impact on our workforce?

What will be the cost and impact on the environment and the planet?

What will be the cost and impact on our local communities?

How can these identified costs and impacts be reduced?

That last question is not often asked. The other iteration to add to your repertoire for each of the first three questions is: what will be the cost and impact if we do nothing?

Another advantage of a Humony workplace is you will foster enhanced buy-in from the people you lead to decisions and actions. This results from participation in execution planning and the cooperative collaboration nature of a harmonious workplace environment. Here is a Buy-In Continuum tool for you to measure the level of buy-in you are achieving with individuals and groups:

Aggressively Opposed

Not in agreement

Wait-and-See / Reluctant Acceptance

Neutral

Willing to Try

Acceptance

Advocate

The same practices apply here as in the Collaboration Continuum in chapter 11. You can only get someone to move one level at a time.

Psychological Safety Leads to Harmony

How team members interact when discussing an issue determines how successful the outcome will be. A dialogic process that harnesses intellectual friction – the sharing and discussing of conflicting ideas – produces optimal outcomes. Such a process enables team members to push and pull, talk and listen, question and answer, respond openly, give and take, brainstorm, toss out ideas (including crazy ones), debate, analyze, and add to the ideas of others. This is harmony and cooperative collaboration at its best. It happens best when psychological safety is abundantly clear and available to all.

Organizational behavior scientist Amy Edmondson of Harvard introduced the concept of team psychological safety. She defined psychological safety as "a shared belief held by members of a team that the team is safe for interpersonal risk taking." Basically, psychological safety means that team members believe that others on the team will not embarrass, reject, or punish them for speaking up. To measure a team's level of psychological safety, Edmondson looks at seven criteria:

1. If you make a mistake on this team, it is often held against you.

2. Members of this team can bring up problems and tough issues.

3. People on this team sometimes reject others for being different.

4. It is safe to take a risk on this team.

5. It is difficult to ask other members of this team for help.

6. No one on this team would deliberately act in a way that undermines my efforts.

7. When working with members of this team, my unique skills and talents are valued and utilized.

High psychological safety drives innovation, creativity, and development. Low psychological safety provokes a sense of fear strong enough that individual survival becomes the primary goal for many, sometimes most, participants. Avoidance of criticism, embarrassment, shame, bullying, and intimidation become the primary objective and driver of disengagement behavior. Guarded responses are more prevalent than the sharing or exploring of unconventional ideas. When it becomes emotionally or politically expensive to "speak outside the box," people stop doing so.

A disharmonious discourse features censoring of one another, self-censoring, withholding of information, reluctant participation, disrespect, discord, withdrawal from the discussion, and other acts of self-preservation. A lack of inclusion results in minimal creativity, innovation, or in-depth thinking and analysis. The first idea to rise to a modicum of acceptability is often the designated and agreed solution. Unfortunately, that solution often needs a course correction or reversal during implementation.

A Harmony Culture is not one where "you agree to disagree" to keep the peace. The desired culture is one where everyone "agrees to understand" one another. Especially about important issues such as sexism, racism, homophobia, and other human rights. A Harmony Culture promotes the right of everyone to be treated equally regardless of race, color, creed, or other human aspects.

This is an issue of morality and human rights, not opinions. Those who have differing views have the right to their views, but not the right to cause disharmony by expressing them in your workplace. It is akin to not being allowed to shout "fire" in a theatre.

No place functions optimally when team members are negatively impacted, individually or collectively, for their uniqueness or personal aspects as human beings.

Learning Culture

Sustainable growth comes when your organization becomes a talent growing business, not a talent buying business. You have to grow talent and not shop for talent. Start developing talent. Stop buying talent.

Learning and development must become core competencies across the organization for sustainable, long-term growth and profitability. To make this happen, learning and development needs to be implanted within the core business functions, led and supported by the Human Capabilities Department (see below). And senior leaders need to stop nuking learning and development budgets as knee-jerk reactions to tough economic conditions. Doing so in 2020 and 2021 was one of the major contributing factors to the Great Resignation of 2021-22.

It is critical to understand what skills will be the foundation for great individuals and teams of the future. While these may differ slightly from industry to industry, I can guarantee you the most important skills are learning how to learn and implementing what you have learned.

Leaders and organizations created a huge people development trench during the pandemic by slashing learning and development budgets. Employees are well aware that these decisions have drastically harmed their professional and personal development. Digging out of this hole will not be easy.

These short-sighted decisions have been an impetus for the Great Resignation and the increased lack of trust in organizations and their senior leaders. Leaders should have known better. It is significantly more cost-effective to create a learning culture and invest in building the skills of current employees than searching, hiring, and onboarding new talent.

Part of a strong learning culture is embedding learning agility across the workforce. Learning agility is the ability to learn from others, from experiences, in formal training sessions, through self-paced programs, and from reflection.

Learning cultures segue from a culture of leaders who "know it all" to one of intellectual humility where everyone, from the top down, is open to learning, committed to improving, and never looks askance or discourages others from having a learning mindset. Intellectual humility means being curious and having an openness to new ideas and sources of information.

The ability of leaders to ask great questions is a skill that spurs learning across teams and organizations. The better the questions leaders ask the more potential pitfalls are uncovered and the greater are the solution options that become available.

Leaders with a "need to be right" can become stuck on a false belief and prolong arguments or move decisions in a wayward direction. Ask yourself: would you rather be right, or would you rather be informed and have a greater understanding? It is always best not to fall into the trap of thinking you know more than you do. Being intellectually humble helps you avoid being overly invested in your own knowledge, ideas, and expertise.

Humony Leaders understand the importance of developing others and themselves. They create cultures where team members are more interested in development than advancement. Not everything is about job titles. Development is an advancement mentality, especially when such development helps ensure the recipient's employability. In adaptable and flexible organizations, less hierarchy means less "advancement" in terms of titles and job codes. However, today's younger workforce knows that responsibilities and personal growth are the true means of professional development and are much more important than titles and job codes.

Managers develop jobs and functionalities. Leaders develop people and careers. They develop people through increased responsibilities and assignments. And through coaching and mentoring.

Life-long learning is an economic imperative for today's times. Toss aside the notion of soft skills. These are people skills and life skills. And not just for leaders; for everybody. One side benefit: people will stay longer when they learn life skills, not just job skills.

Most legacy performance and feedback systems are not built to address today's talent management challenges. Managing talent is the wrong approach. How about motivating talent! Inspiring talent! Unleashing talent! Creating foundational structures to enable talent to grow, flow, flower, and bloom! This is what true performance leadership is all about! This is a true learning culture.

Biggest Step

Perhaps the biggest step you can take to create harmony and a Humony Climate in your workplace is to stop letting jerks survive in your organization. A jerk is:

- Self-serving

- Plays political games

- Focused only on results or on getting promoted to the next level in the organization

There is no room for jerks or bullies in today's organizations, even if they are your highest performer, top salesperson, or most creative individual on the team. Continuing to tolerate such behavior is not conducive to a harmonious environment, nor to your team's long-term, sustainable success.

I am not suggesting you drop them immediately; that would be against the people development principles of Humony Leadership. I do suggest that you set a specific timeframe – six to nine months – for their behavior to improve from tolerable to acceptable. No one is too old to change. Some may be too set in their ways to want to change. But everyone is capable of change, another lesson painfully taught by the pandemic.

While we cannot change people (they have to change themselves), we can clearly point out the impact of their actions on the present and the future. It will be up to them to make a behavior change or not. Either way, they will be accountable and responsible for their decision. Our job as leaders is to explain unambiguously how their current behavior impacts the team, the team's results, their performance, and their relationships with other team members and ourselves.

We also have to unequivocally explain the probable consequences of not changing and the positive benefits likely to occur from changing. No doubt this can be a tough situation, especially when someone with poor people skills is a key performer. But you either have to remove them from interacting with others (very unlikely in today's highly collaborative environments) or remove their damaging behavior. What has been tolerated in the past is no longer acceptable for today and the future.

Human Capabilities Department

It is also time to reconstruct and rethink the Human Resources department. My focus here is an emphasis on *rethinking* how to make this unit of the organization more valuable than currently configured. Currently, the HR department is a necessary evil – for both employees and management. Plus, HR today is too often the compliance department.

As currently structured, the Human Resource Department focuses on ensuring policy and legal compliance, optimizing labor costs, and creating internal procedures for managing the workforce. Even in the areas of recruitment, onboarding, and employee development, the focus is very often on productivity, check-box tasks, cost effectiveness, and how to measure these activities.

How much of recruitment these days is done via automated and self-service processes, and how little includes a human touch or human-to-human interaction? That is what you should be measuring.

How often do employees and potential employees deal with *people* in HR? How often are they directed to access information via intranet pages, an internal app, explanatory videos, or online resume submission sites? What is human about these processes? Very little. How can HR folks identify or understand the challenges people face when there is a dearth of face-to-face *human* interactions?

The technical nuts and bolts of the Human Resources function – payroll, policy creation, compliance, onboarding – are not readily associated with great innovation or enhanced employee engagement. Neither is compliance training such as sexual harassment, antibullying, and DEI programs.

In many ways, some Human Resources entities have become the Human Constraints department. While designed with good intentions or legal requirements in mind, their policies, procedures, and paperwork are more likely to shackle and burden leaders and team members than promote innovation, creativity, flexibility, adaptability, and productivity.

This is not good. Especially when surveys of senior leaders reveal that up to 50% of revenues in 2027 will likely be generated by products and services not currently available. Can you afford to allow HR to throttle the very skills and attributes (innovation, creativity, flexibility, and adaptability) that will drive the new products and services creating half of future revenues?

Unfortunately, HR is often not structured or empowered to make employees better, facilitate their growth, or help them be more engaged with colleagues and work challenges.

I do not have access to Harry Potter's magic wand, so I cannot give you a single formula for restructuring the Human Resources function of your organization. My goal is to prompt your thinking about what is feasible and what might work better for your organization.

There is no one structure for Human Resources that will fit every organization. Over the years, this business unit has evolved from Payroll to the Personnel Department to Human Resources. In some organizations, the evolution has continued with new names like Talent or People. That is the right approach, but a simple name change is not enough. These departments are still mired in policies, procedures, and paperwork. And in many organizations, they have also become the dumping ground for compliance issues.

It is time to move all of the "what gets measured gets down" aspects of HR into Operations or HR Operations. It is time to transform HR from processes to people. HR is a passé name. It is beyond the time to reconstitute the HR Department and its responsibilities.

Now is an optimum time to develop, deploy and leverage the human capabilities of the organization. HR could be a driver of innovation. But it has to stop thinking of senior management as its customer base. Its customer base has to be employees. It needs a marketing mindset that considers its customers' needs first, over its management's desires.

Here is how to start your thinking on what this business unit should become in a Humony Culture environment:

> Start by imagining firing the entire Human Resources team. Letting everyone go. Immediately.

> Then, hire them back 30 minutes later as your Human Capabilities Department.

In doing so, move all of the policy, procedure, payroll, and paperwork responsibilities out of the HR area and into operations. Or create an HR Operations area that works only on these items. Many larger companies have already outsourced payroll and other functions, which clearly indicates this can be done.

Then, re-constitute the Human Resource Department into the Human Capabilities Department. As the Human Capabilities Department, its key responsibility will be to nurture the growth of team members (at all levels). The Human Capabilities team should own the talent development strategy, including the strategy for talent recruitment, onboarding, and culture. Its focus becomes making individuals and groups of individuals (teams, functional levels, hierarchical levels) better. Making people better means helping the company win.

The Human Capabilities team should be tasked with recruiting, onboarding, and developing people's competencies, capabilities, and confidence. Their sole focus is to build the human capabilities that will bring the organization long-term, sustainable success. Remember, the skills of future success are behavioral, not technical. Allow the functional areas to focus on building technical skills. Empower the Human Capabilities team to focus on building behavioral, interpersonal, collaboration, wellbeing, and Humony Leadership skills.

Shifting to people-centric policies, procedures, and processes will help attract and develop talent, including talent pools of those who do not want or are not available for full-time employment. Temporary workers, freelancers, and consultants who are onboarded similar to employees are more likely to be attuned to the organization's values, purpose, and culture than those hired directly by line managers and put immediately to work on projects and assignments. The same goes for the development of these "outside" workers.

And assign the Human Capabilities team the organizational development role of determining how best to implement hybrid, work-from-home, work-from-anywhere, and co-located work teams. Not from a policy standpoint, but from a "what is best for each team member, workgroup, and business results" stance. This would prevent inflexible and restrictive policies from being unilaterally applied across entire organizations. Such policies were early contributors to the Great Resignation. They continue to impact recruitment and employee attrition.

This would also help eliminate team, department, and business unit managers from dictating return-to-office policies simply because they are personally uncomfortable leading remote individuals and teams.

Any Human Capabilities (HC) Business Partners in the organization should be relieved of administrative work. Their number one function should be to help business leaders in the organization drive people development. I would even go so far as to consider having these HC Business Partners drive all career discussions with team members, in conjunction with line managers. These HC Business Partners will also be ideally suited to help line managers and business leaders create tailored and effective development programs for all team members. After all, one cannot expect the Head of Marketing to also be an expert in teaching collaboration skills or emotional intelligence. Or even to know where to look for resources in these areas.

Raising Human Capabilities

Developing the human beings comprising your workforce is the moral and mental starting point for Humony Leadership. Such development includes technical, behavioral, wellness, and life-enhancing skills. Leaders who raise human capabilities across these spectrums will reap incredible benefits, particularly the self-satisfying knowledge that they have endeavored to create a better world for our children and grandchildren to inherit.

This is a leadership responsibility. Even if your organization does not provide sufficient resources to make this happen, it remains your responsibility as a Humony Leader to find ways to do so. Inexpensive and no-cost methods include:

Lunch and learns

Coaching

Mentoring

Guest speakers

Group TedTalk sessions

Attending industry trade shows when locally held

Pro bono speakers

Experience and knowledge sharing among team members

Online development programs

From an organizational perspective, there needs to be a range of creative and innovative programs and policy initiates to help you drive a Humony Culture that creates and rewards long-term employee loyalty. Here are a few thought starters for you, in no particular order:

Provide growth pathways with continuous growth opportunities for all as a foundation. These can segue into career pathways for those who choose to build their careers with your organization.

Transform annual raise cycles to more frequent pay reviews. Grant immediate rewards for those who complete formal training or self-administered learning programs and then demonstrate the ability to implement what they have learned. Want people to buy-into continuous development? Then reward them for doing so.

Eliminate Ranking Systems and the time-consuming paperwork and discussions around the annual employee ranking process. No one likes these. No one really benefits from this process. And they are not worth the time, effort, and angst they cause. Forced ranking is a legacy of the 1980s managing people construct. Like most things from the 1980s, this system is best forgotten.

Tenure Awards of $1000 for every year of service. Someone who has been with the organization for five years would be making a $5000/year higher salary than someone just starting in the same or similar position. Pay this either as an annual bonus (on the anniversary of their starting date) or build it into the monthly payroll.

Link Dividends and Salaries so that employees are as valued as shareholders (especially those non-human institutional investors). Every time you raise dividends, your human workforce receives an equal raise of the same percentage. Increase dividends by 3% and all employees (and contract workers) also receive a 3% raise on their base salaries or fees.

Create policies that are more human-centric, such as eliminating those three-day bereavement policies. We have certainly learned during the pandemic that people need more time to bereave, especially for close loved ones.

Promote cooperative collaboration with

rewards and incentives linked to group outcomes and collaborating with others.

Adaptable and flexible teams along the Hollywood approach, leaving the actors (team members) as the stars.

Leadership evaluations focus on a leader's ability to form and lead teams and produce team-driven results. Knock back the concept that the role of leaders is to run a functional department. There is nothing agile or flexible about departments. Focus on teams, teams, teams! Also, evaluate leaders on their ability to create multiple plans, not just how well they execute a single plan.

Contracts for everyone, not just executives. Hire all non-hourly employees on 18 to 24 month employment contracts. This is guaranteed to create more motivated team members when their contracts are starting to expire (for proof, see how much better NBA players perform when their contracts are up for renewal). As contract tenures come to a close, team members can recontract for their current roles and responsibilities, look for other opportunities within the organization that interest them, or take their skill sets elsewhere. Everyone knows when the tenure is about to expire, so there are no surprises and an opportunity for all stakeholders to work together. These contracts can include performance standards (turn IT Service Level Agreements into Personal Deliverable Agreements). This will make you rethink job scopes and job descriptions. Plus, both parties will work to ensure the right resources are available for success.

Work/Life Harmony is not about balancing work and life. The future is about blending life and work. When this is understood and handled appropriately your future organization will comprise teams and managers still dedicated to your organizational purpose and mission. If handled incorrectly, you will wind up with a cohort of freelancers and gig workers not necessarily attuned to your culture and values.

These concepts will change your organization and your human workforce for the better. They will help you create a Humony Culture, led by Humony Leaders, capable of creating long-term, sustainable success for your organization. The chart below highlights some other Humony Culture aspects you and your team members will experience.

Harmony Culture Signs

I love this quote from Minouche Shafik, Director of London School of Economics, "*In the past jobs were about muscles, now they're about brains, but in the future, they'll be about the heart.*" I would only disagree to say that the future of work (which is here now) requires both brains and hearts. That is what you need to hire. And those are the components of the human workforce that leaders need to understand, motivate, and lead.

When you enable the brains and hearts of your team members, you will create Humony Cultures with the following features, characteristics, and advantages over the standard pre-pandemic methods of running organizations:

The Pre-pandemic Normal	Harmony Culture
Work set hours (9-5)	Work any time as personally suited
Focus on accomplishing tasks during working hours	Focus on accomplishing tasks and adding value
Perform work in the employer's designated workplace	Work anywhere as personally suited
Blame and shame culture	Psychological safety in place Mistakes happen, providing learning opportunities
Company-owned desktop computers stay onsite	Use mobile devices and cloud storage
Climb the corporate ladder at the company's pace	Create your own career ladder at your own pace
Routine and boring work	Customized work requiring thoughts and input, often collaboratively
Tendency to hoard information	Willingly sharing information
Little or no voice in decisions	Team members actively engaged in determining execution plans

Focus on functional expertise	Focus on creating people leaders
Communicate via memos and emails	Communicate via collaboration technologies and open discussions
SMEs are knowledge-based experts	SMEs focus on continuous and adaptive learning
Corporate-driven learning events	Personalized learning and continuous learning opportunities
Occasional upskilling of technical skills for a portion of the workforce	Continuous learning culture applicable to all
Forced collaboration	Cooperative collaboration
Conflict and drama are readily apparent	Conflict is turned into collaboration
Us vs. Them identities	Kindness, compassion, and understanding between all employees
Status driven	Equality for all
Abusive bosses	Trust and respect exhibited by leaders and returned in kind by team members
Lack of acknowledgment	Leaders express gratitude and recognize efforts

Humony Climates and Humony Cultures will enable people to find and leverage valuable sources of nourishment, passion, and purpose within their jobs, workplaces and working environments.

Humony Climates and Humony Cultures are places of harmony enabling people to unthrottled their mental, emotional, and physical energies and attain the increased creativity, thinking, and productivity that comes from flow states.

Who wouldn't want to work in such an environment?

Who wouldn't want to lead such an environment?

Is this attainable? In the words of Robert F. Kennedy shared at the beginning of this book "why not?"

All it takes is your imagination, determination, and sustained effort.

Tend to the people and they will tend to the business.
John Maxwell

CHAPTER 14

Benefits of Humony

Trust men and they will be true to you;
treat them greatly and they will show themselves great.
Ralph Waldo Emerson

To create a better world, we must become better people, better leaders, and better people leaders.

Humony Leadership will help you evolve into a better person, leader, and people leader. You will become a leader who is admired. A leader who is trusted. A leader that people look to for motivation, coaching, and direction. And a leader destined for a rewarding and fulfilling leadership career.

Benefits

Who benefits from the Humony Leadership approach?

> Team Members – by being treated as humans and not staff or "resources"

> Organizations – through greatly reduced employee attrition, absenteeism, presenteeism, and associated medical and insurance costs

> Business Results – through greater creativity, productivity, and employee engagement

> Leaders – through attaining greater results and more harmonious workplaces and an increase in

leadership wellbeing

Society – through an increase in kindness and a decrease in public displays of incivility

These benefits create thriving organizations comprising thriving leaders and employees.

Thriving

One of the biggest benefits for Humony Leaders is a sense of thriving and wellbeing.

Thriving means being successful and happy. It implies a sense of flourishing, being fully alive, living life to the full, and firing on all cylinders. It also means being at ease with life, full of contentment, and having a sense of balance and calmness.

The wellbeing aspect of Humony Leadership flows across all four dimensions of your human experience – mental, emotional, spiritual, and physical. Incorporating the mindsets, skills, and behaviors of a Humony Leader will bring you less stress, enhance your emotional intelligence capabilities, and improve your working relationships. You will also have a greater understanding and respect for your fellow human beings with whom you interact, work, and lead.

Improved Workplace Climate

Culture happens at an organizational level. Climate happens at the team level and is driven by the team leader.

The benefits of Humony Leadership on workplace climate include:

- Engaged employees
- Increased productivity

- Higher workforce retention

- Finite and specific boundaries established

- Clear-cut resolutions of drama and conflict

- Team members are constantly learning

- Empowered individuals and teams (with agreed decision rights)

In turn, this will lead to:

- Reduced employee attrition, absenteeism, presenteeism, sick days

- Lower health insurance costs for your organization

- Lower unemployment payments / taxes / contributions

- Higher employee engagement, which results in (according to Gallup):

  - ➤ 41% fewer quality defects

  - ➤ 48% fewer safety incidents

  - ➤ 26% less shrinkage from employee theft or waste

  - ➤ 65% less staff turnover (in low employee turnover organizations)

  - ➤ 25% less staff turnover (in high employee turnover organizations)

  - ➤ 37% less absenteeism

And perhaps the best benefit of all is more workplace environments will segue into kinder, more harmonious workplaces. Additionally, these will also become places enabling smart, intelligent, engaged people to do great work.

To paraphrase the Peter Drucker quote at the start of chapter one:

> *Only three things happen in organizations – friction, confusion, and underperformance; all aspects of sustainable success require Humony Leaders.*

Remember, good leaders are good at either leading for results or leading people. Great leaders excel at doing both. Great leaders achieve progress through the involvement and actions of others. Humony Leaders are great leaders who achieve progress through the involvement and actions of others while being people-centric in their mindsets, behaviors, and actions. Such leaders can be found – and need to be found – at all levels of organizations.

To create a better world, we must become better people, better leaders, and better people leaders. We need leaders creating a kinder, more peaceful world. A better world for our grandchildren to inherit. It starts with each of us.

I alone cannot change the world,
but I can cast a shadow across the waters
to create many ripples.
Mother Teresa

Quotes Related to Humony Leadership

Treat people as if they were what they ought to be and you will help them become what they are capable of becoming.
Johann Wolfgang von Goethe

People want to know they matter and they want to be treated as people. That's the new talent contract.
Pamela Stroko

Everyone wants to be appreciated, so if you appreciate someone, don't keep it a secret.
Mary Kay Ash

Those who have high thoughts are ever striving; they are not happy to remain in the same place.
Buddha

I studied the lives of great men and famous women, and I found that the men and women who got to the top were those who did the jobs they had in hand, with everything they had of energy and enthusiasm and hard work.
Harry S. Truman

Three secrets to success: be willing to learn new things. Be able to assimilate new information quickly. Be able to get along with and work with other people.
Sally Ride

The only limit to our realization of tomorrow will be our doubts of today.
Franklin D. Roosevelt

*We need to accept that we won't always make the right deci-
sions, that we'll screw up royally sometimes – understanding
that failure is not the opposite of success; it's a part of success.*
Arianna Huffington

*You cannot create long-term value for the shareholder unless
you create long-term value for the employees and the communities you serve.*
Howard Schultz

Invest in yourself, in your education. There's nothing better.
Sylvia Porter

*I do not think that there is any other quality so essential to suc-
cess of any kind as the quality of perseverance.*
John D. Rockefeller

*Take responsibility for yourself...because no one's going to take
responsibility for you.*
Tyra Banks

*There are no hopeless situations, only those who have grown
helpless about them.*
Clare Boothe Luce

*You will succeed if you persevere, and you will find a joy in
overcoming obstacles, a delight in climbing rugged paths,
which you would perhaps never know if you did not sometime
slip backward.*
Helen Keller

*If the rate of change of your employees exceeds the rate of
change of your talent strategies, the end is near.*
Steve Cadigan

We may encounter many defeats, but we must not be defeated. It may even be necessary to encounter the defeat so that we can know who we are. So that we can see, "oh, that happened and I rose. I did get knocked down flat in front of the whole world, and I rose. I didn't run away. I rose right where I'd been knocked down."
Maya Angelou

Today a reader, tomorrow a leader.
Margaret Fuller

Do not wait for leaders. Do it alone, person to person.
Mother Teresa

You manage things; you lead people.
Rear Admiral Grace Murray Hopper

Leadership is about making others better as a result of your presence and making sure that impact lasts in your absence.
Sheryl Sandberg

Good leaders organize and align people around what the team needs to do. Great leaders motivate and inspire people with why they're doing it. That's purpose. And that's the key to achieving something truly transformational.
Marilyn Hewson

I measure my own success as a leader by how well the people who work for me succeed.
Maria Shi

The goal of many leaders is to get people to think more highly of the leader. The goal of a great leader is to help people think more highly of themselves.
J. Carla Northcutt

Don't limit yourself. Many people limit themselves to what they think they can do. You can go as far as your mind lets you. What you believe, you can achieve.
Mary Kay Ash

Learn. Know what you didn't know before.
Eileen Fisher

It's okay to admit what you don't know. It's okay to ask for help. And it's more than okay to listen to the people you lead – in fact, it's essential.
Mary Barra

When people go to work, they shouldn't have to leave their hearts at home.
Betty Bender

Culture is about performance, and making people feel good about how they contribute to the whole.
Tracy Streckenbach

If you don't give people a chance to fail, you won't innovate. If you want to be an innovative company, allow people to make mistakes.
Indra Nooyi

In the absence of feedback, people will fill in the blanks with a negative. They will assume you don't like them.
Pat Summitt

We are not what we know but what we are willing to learn.
Mary Catherine Bateson

The task of leadership is not to put greatness into humanity, but to elicit it, for the greatness is already there.
John Buchan

Don't ever wait around for someone else to tell you how to develop yourself.
April Arnzen

The purpose of our lives is to give birth to the best which is within us.
Marianne Williamson

All of the great leaders have had one characteristic in common: it was the willingness to confront unequivocally the major anxiety of their people in their time. This, and not much else, is the essence of leadership.
John Kenneth Galbraith

A positive attitude gives you power over your circumstances instead of your circumstances having power over you.
Joyce Meyer

The greatest discovery of my generation is that human beings can alter their lives by altering their attitudes of mind.
William James

A different world cannot be built by indifferent people.
Peter Marshall

I alone cannot change the world, but I can cast a stone across the waters to create many ripples.
Mother Teresa

It is more important to know where you are going than to get there quickly.
Mabel Newcomber

Growth and comfort do not exist. That's true for people, companies, and nations.
Ginni Rometty

When you take risks, you learn that there will be times when you succeed and there will be times when you fail, and both are equally important.
Ellen DeGeneres

We are a performance-driven organization, but we have to lead the company through the lens of humanity.
Howard Schultz

In moments of pessimism, remember five great truths:
> *1) everything happens for a reason,*
> *2) pain is a source of growth,*
> *3) complaining and worrying never helps,*
> *4) patience does work, and*
> *5) to always keep going is better than stopping or standing still.*

Adriana Fuentes Díaz

Steven Howard Quotes on Leadership

Never stop learning because life never stops teaching.

Great leaders are not afraid of mistakes or failures. They are only afraid of not learning from mistakes and failures.

Peace of mind in the workplace is not the absence of conflict but the ability to cope with it without drama or victimization.

Leadership is not a position, title, or spot on an organizational chart. Leadership is a skill to be developed, practiced, and enhanced.

It is not what happens that defines you; it is what you do next.

Don't be a prisoner of your past. Be the architect of your future.

You are your life's most important variable.

You are the only one holding you back.

Progress is less about speed and much more about direction.

When feedback is combined with forgiveness, leaders are more likely to prompt and motivate changes that result in better performance and improved behavior.

One of the greatest gifts a leader can give to team members is to help them find and grow their talents.

Continuous training of your employees, especially in the "soft skills" areas of teamwork, collaboration, and working across boundaries, is the key to scaling every part of your business.

Leaders who don't listen will eventually be surrounded by people unwilling to speak and contribute.

The true measure of team leadership is not about how many team members are working but how well they are working together.

A team is not a group of people who work together. A team is a group of people working together towards a shared outcome who trust and respect each other.

Your greatness does not need to be proven. Only exhibited.

Mistakes are an iterative part of life. Mistakes will not define who you are. Responding and recovering from mistakes do.

Wisdom is not about knowing all the answers. Wisdom is asking the right questions of the right person or people.

No one is unflawed or perfect. Flaws are charming and likable. Accept your flaws. Admit your mistakes. Doing so will not hurt you. But their denial and cover-up will.

As you move into higher leadership positions, your network is part of your net worth to your organization and your team.

Don't base your desired outcome only on income. Do some good.

Acknowledgments

First, to the core group of individuals with whom I exchanged the initial concepts of *Humony Leadership* and who provided valuable feedback: Adriana Fuentes Díaz, Ali Shami, Ed Cohen, Gregg Ward, Jorge Gibbons, Ken Somers, Mac Bogert, Paco Partida, Steinar Hjelle, and Todd Taylor.

A very special thanks and appreciation goes to Steve Cadigan, who not only wrote the wonderful Foreword to this book, but also provided valuable feedback and ideas that strengthened and enhanced the concepts of Humony Leadership.

Special thanks to Ed Cohen, my co-host of the online TV Talk Shows *StriveXL* and *ThriveXL,* and Hector Castañeda for the wonderful design concepts he created for the book cover.

I want to recognize and thank the leaders with whom I have worked whose thoughts and behaviors have influenced my thinking on leadership: April Arnzen (Micron Technology), Deirdre Ball (Reader's Digest and The Financial Times), Al Bond (Texas Instruments), Nancy Elder (formerly MasterCard, now NY Mets), Goh Geok Ling (Texas Instruments), Jonathon Gould (MasterCard), Steinar Hjelle (formerly Micron Technology, now Boise Cascade), Ron Mahoney (Texas Instruments), William Malloy (Forum Corporation), Rodrigo S. Martineli (formerly HPE, now Rackspace Technology), Shisho Matsushima (TIME

Magazine), David McAuliffe (TIME Magazine), Ed Morrett (Texas Instruments), Ralph Oliva (Texas Instruments), André Sekulic (MasterCard), David Smith (Citibank), Rana Talwar (Citibank), Georgette Tan (MasterCard), Todd Taylor (formerly HPE, now the University of Notre Dame), and Frank Walters (Texas Instruments).

I would also like to thank those who have provided me an opportunity to present Humony Leadership at their events:

Angela Romeo at Zaccato Concept in Atlanta

Cecilia Zaragaza Peña and Astrid Manjarrez Rojas at Business 4.0 in Monterrey, Mexico

Julianne O'Brien, Manager Talent Development and the LDP (Learn Develop Perform) program at AbbVie.

About the Author

Steven Howard is an award-winning author of 22 leadership, marketing, and management books and the editor of nine professional and personal development books in the *Project You* series.

His book *Better Decisions Better Thinking Better Outcomes: How to go from Mind Full to Mindful Leadership*, received a Silver Award from the Nonfiction Authors Association. He also wrote *Leadership Lessons from the Volkswagen Saga*, which won three prestigious publishing industry awards (2017 Independent Press Award, National Indie Excellence Award, and San Francisco Book Festival Award).

Steven is also the author of *Great Leadership Words of Wisdom* and co-author of *Strong Women Speak on Leadership, Success and Living Well: Lessons for Life from Strong Women Through the Ages.*

His corporate career covered a wide variety of fields and experiences, including Regional Marketing Director for Texas Instruments Asia-Pacific, Regional Director South Asia for TIME Magazine, Global Account Director at BBDO Advertising handling an international airline account, and VP Marketing for Citibank's Consumer Banking Group.

In the past 25 years he has mentored, coached, and trained over 10,000 leaders in Asia, Australia, Africa, Europe, Mexico, and North America.

He brings a truly international, cross-cultural perspective to his clients, having lived in the USA for over 30 years, in Singapore for 21 years, and in Australia for 12 years. He currently resides in Mexico City.

Contact Details:
Email: steven@CalienteLeadership.com
Twitter: @stevenbhoward | @GreatLeadershp
LinkedIn: www.linkedin.com/in/stevenbhoward
Website: www.CalienteLeadership.com
Website: www.HumonyLeadership.com

Printed in Great Britain
by Amazon

11991854R00188